A-LEVEL YEAR 2
STUDENT GUIDE

OCR

Economics

Macroeconomics 2

Sam Dobin

PHILIP ALLAN FOR
HODDER
EDUCATION
AN HACHETTE UK COMPANY

Philip Allan, an imprint of Hodder Education, an Hachette UK company, Blenheim Court, George Street, Banbury, Oxfordshire OX16 5BH

Orders

Bookpoint Ltd, 130 Park Drive, Milton Park, Abingdon, Oxfordshire OX14 4SB

tel: 01235 827827

fax: 01235 400401

e-mail: education@bookpoint.co.uk

Lines are open 9.00 a.m.–5.00 p.m., Monday to Saturday, with a 24-hour message answering service. You can also order through the Hodder Education website: www.hoddereducation.co.uk

© Sam Dobin 2016

ISBN 978-1-4718-5783-6

First printed 2016

Impression number 5 4 3 2 1

Year 2020 2019 2018 2017 2016

This Guide has been written specifically to support students preparing for the OCR A-level Economics examinations. The content has been neither approved nor endorsed by OCR and remains the sole responsibility of the author.

Cover photo: Iakov Kalinin

Typeset by Integra Software Services Pvt. Ltd., Pondicherry, India

Printed in Italy

Hachette UK's policy is to use papers that are natural, renewable and recyclable products and made from wood grown in sustainable forests. The logging and manufacturing processes are expected to conform to the environmental regulations of the country of origin.

Contents

Content Guidance

Questions & Answers

■ Getting the most from this book

Exam tips

Advice on key points in the text to help you learn and recall content, avoid pitfalls and polish your exam technique in order to boost your grade.

Knowledge check

Rapid-fire questions throughout the Content Guidance section to check your understanding.

Knowledge check answers

1 Turn to the back of the book for the Knowledge check answers.

Summaries

■ Each core topic is rounded off by a bullet-list summary for quick-check reference of what you need to know.

Exam-style questions

Commentary on the questions

Tips on what you need to do to gain full marks, indicated by the icon **e**

Sample student answers

Practise the questions, then look at the student answers that follow.

Commentary on sample student answers

Find out how many marks each answer would be awarded in the exam and then read the comments (preceded by the icon **e**) following each student answer. Annotations that link back to points made in the student answers show exactly how and where marks are gained or lost.

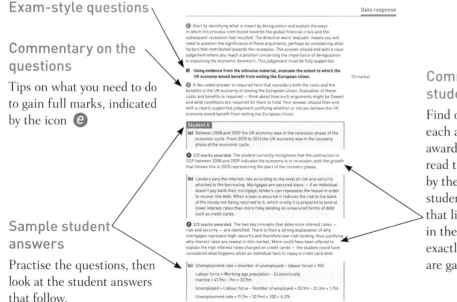

■ About this book

This guide is designed to prepare you for the A-level OCR Macroeconomics exam and the A-level OCR Themes in Economics exam. It includes sample questions and answers to prepare you for both papers. In addition to the content covered here, you will need to be familiar with the content in *Student Guide 2* to sit the A-level Macroeconomics exam and the content in *Student Guides 1, 2* and *3* in order to sit the A-level Themes in Economics exam.

The guide is split into two sections:

Content Guidance

This section explains the core macroeconomics concepts required to excel in this course. This can be split into five broad topic areas:

- Economic policy objectives and indicators of macroeconomic performance
- Aggregate demand and aggregate supply
- The application of policy instruments
- The global context
- The financial sector

You should make sure you have fully mastered all of the content in this guide before progressing to the practice questions. Use the knowledge checks as you work your way through the guide to test your understanding and take on board the comments to avoid falling into the traps that most commonly result in students losing marks. At the end of each topic area there is a bullet-pointed summary of the content covered — if you are unable to offer a detailed explanation of any part of this you should read the section again to clear up any misunderstanding.

Questions & Answers

This section begins by setting out the format of the exam papers, giving you advice on how long to spend on each question and offering important tips on how to maximise your marks on the different elements of the paper. It also explains the levels system used to mark essays.

This is followed by a series of sample questions. After all of these questions there are some example answers from students. You should practise all of these questions yourself and compare your answers to these while reading the detailed comments to improve your understanding of what is required to achieve full marks.

Content Guidance

■ Economic policy objectives and indicators of macroeconomic performance

Economic growth and development

Economic development is a process that results in improved standards of living for inhabitants of a country. While economic growth is the most obvious mechanism through which this can be achieved, this is not the only dimension of development — a country experiencing the wrong sort of economic growth that impacts only part of the population may not be developing, as large sections of society could still be living in poverty. In 2000 the United Nations agreed on the Millennium Development Goals, which act as targets for each less developed country (LDC), as priorities for development. These were:

- Eradicate extreme poverty
- Achieve universal primary education
- Promote gender equality and empower women
- Reduce child mortality
- Improve maternal health
- Combat HIV/AIDS, malaria and other diseases
- Ensure environmental sustainability
- Develop a global partnership for development.

Increasing real gross domestic product (GDP) per capita is clearly a route through which some of these goals can be achieved.

Measuring economic development

GNI per capita

Gross national income (GNI) per capita is one of the main measures of economic development. It is preferable to using GDP per capita as it includes net income from abroad, which can be significant for some developing nations relying on remittances from citizens working in developed economies. It can be calculated by dividing GNI by the population to give an estimate of average income in the country.

This measure is relatively straightforward to calculate and is well established, meaning it is an indicator that is available for almost every country in the world. This enables comparisons to be made between countries. For example, in 2014 GNI per

> **Exam tip**
>
> Economic growth is considered a necessary but not sufficient condition for development to take place. This means that development will not be achieved without economic growth but that economic growth alone does not necessarily lead to development if it does nothing to reduce poverty or improve standards of education and health.

capita stood at $630 in Mozambique and $55,200 in the USA. From this data we can conclude that material standards of living are significantly higher in the USA than in Mozambique.

However, there are a number of weaknesses with this measure of development which need to be recognised:

- **Exchange rate problems** — to enable comparisons to be made between countries, GNI per capita is converted into US dollars at the official exchange rates. However, in many cases these exchange rates do not represent the true value of the currency in terms of the local purchasing power of incomes. This is because in many countries the government manipulates the value of the currency — an example of this is China, where the currency is deliberately undervalued to make exports price competitive. Even when left to the free market the exchange rate is determined by the price of internationally traded goods, which will be different to the standard basket of goods purchased by most consumers. To overcome this problem an alternative set of estimates — GNI per capita based on purchasing power parity (PPP) — has been produced to more accurately reflect the relative purchasing power of incomes in different countries. In general, these data suggest that the gap between low-income and high-income countries is not as big as initially suggested by the US dollar estimates.
- **The informal sector** — in many LDCs there is a significant amount of economic activity in the informal sector. This may be illegal activity or legitimate activity that is not marketised, such as subsistence farming. Because GNI includes only recorded transactions, this measure is therefore likely to miss out much economic activity which takes place, meaning it does not give an accurate reflection of a country's output.
- **Income distribution** — GNI per capita provides data on average incomes but gives no sense of how income is distributed. GNI per capita could be rising as a result of a small group of wealthy individuals getting significantly wealthier while the majority of the population are getting a little poorer. Such a rise in GNI per capita would not represent economic development. Therefore, GNI per capita does not provide information on living standards across society.
- **Social indicators** — standard of living depends upon more than just the material resources available in an economy. Clearly how such resources are used is important — quality of life is likely to be higher in a country using its income to develop its education and healthcare provision in comparison with a country using its income for military expenditure. The quality of the environment in which individuals live is also important and is something that can be distorted by GNI data — production that causes pollution can worsen individuals' quality of life, but the cost of any policies designed to clean up this pollution, known as defensive expenditure, will actually enhance GNI, even though the net effect of the production is to worsen standard of living.

HDI and other social indicators

The Human Development Index (HDI) is an alternative indicator of economic development designed to deal with some of the criticisms of purely income-based measures. It has three main components, shown in Table 1.

Knowledge check 1

Using the PPP measure of GNI per capita, average income was $55,860 in the USA and $1,170 in Mozambique. How does this change the conclusions you may have reached about the relative standards of living in the two countries based on the US dollar estimates?

Table 1

Component	Justification for inclusion	Measurement
Resources	The resources available in an economy dictate the potential standard of living available.	GNI per capita (in PPP%) — a proxy for individuals' material standard of living.
Knowledge	Being able to make good use of available resources is crucial in achieving high standards of living.	Mean years of schooling (reflects past investment in education) and expected years of schooling (reflects current state of education).
Lifespan	Living long enough to make use of an economy's resources will have a significant impact on standard of living.	Life expectancy — a proxy for individuals' health.

The measurements are combined to produce a composite index ranging between 0 and 1. The closer the HDI value is to 1, the higher the level of human development.

Economists continue to debate how important economic growth is to economic development. On the one hand, economic growth can directly contribute to improved education and life expectancy. But on the other hand, focusing on improved education and health can lead to higher economic growth. What is clear is that the GNI and HDI measures produce very different pictures of development. Countries such as Brazil and South Africa, for example, have seen rapidly rising GNI per capita but are much lower on the HDI ranking because of issues concerning inequality and poor life expectancy.

Given the difficulties in reflecting economic development in one statistic, economists continue to use a range of different measures to assess development. In recent years the Genuine Progress Indicator (GPI) has become increasingly popular. This is comprised of 26 components covering economic, environmental and social factors and is designed to produce a broader measure of development than that provided by the HDI.

Economic growth and happiness

It may seem obvious that economic growth makes people happier — increased disposable income does after all enable individuals to enjoy a higher material standard of living. However, economist Richard Easterlin found that, while happiness and income appear to be correlated at a point in time, happiness does not appear to increase as income increases over time. This is known as the Easterlin paradox. It suggests that an individual's happiness is determined more by their income relative to others around them than by their absolute level of income — this fits with traditional labour market theory, which argues that in wage negotiations individuals are more concerned with maintaining differentials with other occupations or roles within the occupation than achieving a particular absolute wage.

It is also clear to see that there are circumstances under which individuals' happiness will fall as economic growth occurs. This is particularly true if the growth occurs as a result of longer working hours, which can increase stress levels and reduce leisure time.

Exam tip

It is important to recognise that the HDI is not a fully inclusive measure of economic development. There are many other factors that contribute to standard of living which are not included, such as average working hours, crime rates and the quality of the environment.

Promoting economic development

The structure of economic activity

In 1960 economic historian Walt Rostow proposed a model outlining the five stages of economic growth that developed countries had passed through. This can be illustrated in Figure 1.

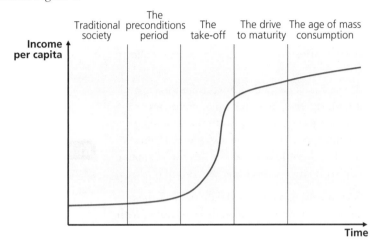

Figure 1 The stages of economic growth

The stages can be explained as follows:

- **Traditional society** — most of the production takes place in the **primary sector**, with agriculture dominating economic activity. Investment and productivity are low.
- **The preconditions period** — labour productivity begins to increase, which allows resources to be diverted to enable **secondary sector** production to develop. During this phase there is investment in infrastructure to provide the foundations for future economic growth.
- **The take-off** — a 20–30-year period of rapid economic growth, fuelled by the emergence of entrepreneurs taking risks in rapidly expanding manufacturing output. Investment is high in this period.
- **The drive to maturity** — a period of self-sustaining growth where economic activity becomes more diversified as a result of continued high investment. **Tertiary sector** production begins to occur.
- **The age of mass consumption** — the economy is fully diversified, output per head continues to rise and consumption now accounts for a higher proportion of GDP.

Rostow argued that some countries remained trapped in the first stage of economic growth, largely because of the high dependence on the primary sector experienced by many LDCs. Because agricultural productivity tends to be low, this means income per head remains low and there are insufficient funds to generate the investment needed for development to take place. Moreover, given the declining terms of trade agricultural producers face in the modern world, alongside the inherent volatility in agricultural prices, individuals in economies reliant on agriculture face uncertain futures.

Primary sector Production using natural resources, including the extraction of raw materials and the growing of crops.

Secondary sector Production of manufactured goods.

Tertiary sector Production of services, which may include the quaternary sector (involving intellectual services).

ODA and international trade

Overseas development assistance (ODA) is provided through the Development Assistance Committee of the OECD. There are a number of reasons why developed nations dedicate significant amounts to ODA each year:

- **Humanitarian motives** — ODA can be used to provide access to clean water and improve healthcare to reduce child mortality rates and increase life expectancy.
- **Political motives** — in some circumstances countries will give aid to nations that are not necessarily the world's poorest nations because of their foreign policy objectives.
- **To promote trade** — aid can provide the funds needed for investment to expand international trade, which can benefit both the recipient and donor countries. Trade is essential for developing nations as it gives them access to the capital they need to grow that they cannot produce themselves while also giving them markets of high-income consumers to sell to. For the donor countries the economic development of LDCs can provide them with larger export markets to sell to.

At a 1974 meeting of the United Nations countries agreed to dedicate 0.7% of their GDP to ODA. However, progress towards achieving this has been disappointing, with only a handful of Scandinavian countries such as Sweden, Norway and Denmark meeting the target.

Despite the investment in ODA, there is debate over its effectiveness, with a 1997 World Bank study finding that there is no evidence that such assistance improves the growth rate or quality of economic policies in the recipient nations, except in situations where the economic management of the country was already sound prior to receipt of the aid.

There are a number of possible reasons why aid may be ineffective:

- LDCs have insufficient resources to be able to use the aid effectively.
- Governments in LDCs are sometimes inefficient or corrupt, meaning funds are not used to benefit the population.
- The sums of money donated are insufficient to deal with such fundamental problems in LDCs.
- Aid is sometimes given as part of an aid-to-trade deal, where the recipient is required to purchase goods from the donor country at inflated prices as a condition of the aid.
- When aid is tied to specific projects this means the funds cannot always be used to deal with the country's top priorities, with donor countries sometimes tying aid to 'prestige' projects.
- Receipt of aid can cause a country's exchange rate to rise, worsening the international price competitiveness of exports. This is known as Dutch disease.

International organisations

There are a number of international organisations that exist to offer support to developing nations:

- **International Monetary Fund (IMF)** — acts as a bank for central banks, providing short-term financial assistance to enable countries to finance balance of

Knowledge check 2

ODA can come in the form of bilateral or multilateral aid. What is the difference between the two?

payments deficits. Such financial assistance usually comes with conditions, such as implementing contractionary fiscal and monetary policy.

- **World Bank** — provides long-term funding for projects that promote development. Such funding is provided at commercial interest rates in situations in which commercial banks would see the lending as too risky.
- **World Trade Organization (WTO)** — exists to promote free trade, encouraging the removal of barriers to trade between countries and in doing so improving developing countries' ability to sell their products abroad.

Institutions such as the IMF and the World Bank have encouraged developing countries to adopt a series of policies known as the Washington Consensus, which primarily consists of market reforms to strengthen the role of markets in the economy. Economists have in recent years argued that the Washington Consensus presents a simplified view of the steps needed to achieve economic development as it ignores the importance of stable political and financial institutions. Moreover, the path China has taken to growth, blending markets with significant state control of assets, provides further evidence that there are a number of different ways in which development can be achieved.

Income distribution and welfare

Income is the flow of money over a period of time, including wages and interest from capital investment. Income inequality measures the extent to which income is distributed across the population — a high degree of income inequality means there are big differences between the earnings of those at the top and those at the bottom of the distribution of income. Income inequality can lead to poverty, which can be categorised into two types:

- **Absolute poverty** — a situation in which individuals have insufficient income to purchase the basic necessities for survival (food, water and shelter).
- **Relative poverty** — a situation in which individuals have insufficient income to participate in the normal social life of a country, defined as having an income level below 50% of median adjusted household disposable income.

However, there are a number of reasons why income inequality is not necessarily the best measure of inequality:

- Absolute household income levels do not account for differences in household composition. Using equivalence scales can help solve this problem. For example, if a couple with no children is given a value of 1 and each child in the household adds 0.25 to the equivalence scale, then a couple with three children would be assigned a value of 1.75. Dividing household income by the equivalence scale (which in this instance would turn a £50,000 household income into £28,571) produces an equivalised income, which allows for meaningful comparisons to be made between households.
- People tend to smooth consumption over their lifetimes, meaning differences in expenditure may be a better indicator of inequality than differences in income.
- Differences in income can be partly offset by government policy. In countries where there are generous benefits systems and state provision of lots of services there may be little inequality, even when the distribution of income is unequal.

Exam tip

While organisations such as the WTO should theoretically make it easier for developing nations to compete, it is important to note that they are weakened by the vested interest that exists — ultimately these organisations are run by developed countries which often set policy to suit their own interests.

Knowledge check 3

Which type of poverty is most common in the UK? Why is this?

Wealth inequality is an alternative way to measure inequality. Wealth is defined as an accumulated stock of assets, such as savings and property. In the UK the distribution of wealth is more unequal than the distribution of income.

Measuring inequality

Income ratios

One method of measuring income inequality is to rank households in order of their incomes and then calculate the share of total household income that goes to a particular group of earners. The 90:10 ratio measures the ratio of the income earned by the top 10% of earners to the income earned by the bottom 10% of earners. In the USA the ratio is approximately 16, indicating that the richest 10% of earners earn 16 times more than the poorest 10% of earners. Sometimes earners are grouped into quintiles, i.e. in 20% groupings.

The Lorenz curve

The Lorenz curve provides a graphical measure of income inequality. In Figure 2 the line of equality represents a situation in which income is perfectly distributed within a country — for example, the bottom 20% of households account for 20% of national income.

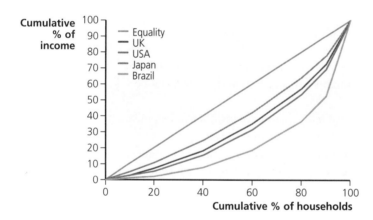

Figure 2 Lorenz curves

The further away the Lorenz curve is from the line of equality, the more unequal the distribution of income is. In Japan, for example, the 40% of households at the bottom of the distribution of income account for approximately 23% of national income while the 10% of households at the top of the distribution of income account for approximately 21% of national income.

The Gini coefficient

The Gini coefficient provides a numerical measure of income inequality which allows for comparisons to be made between countries. It is calculated using the following equation:

$$\text{Gini coefficient} = \frac{\text{Area A}}{\text{Area A} + \text{B}}$$

Knowledge check 4

Rank the countries in Figure 2 according to how evenly distributed income is, starting with the country with the most equal distribution of income.

These areas are illustrated in Figure 3. The calculation will produce an answer between 0 and 1. The closer the coefficient is to zero, the more equal the distribution of income is — if the Lorenz curve was on the line of equality, Area A would not exist, giving a Gini coefficient of zero. The closer the coefficient is to one, the more unequal the distribution of income is.

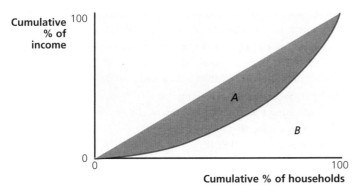

Figure 3 Calculating the Gini coefficient

The further the Lorenz curve is from the line of the equality the larger Area A will be, the closer the Gini coefficient will be to one and the more unequal the distribution of income will be.

Causes of inequality and poverty

Inequality and poverty can be explained by a number of factors:

- **Labour market factors** — given that wages are the biggest component of income, differences in wage rates provide the primary explanation for income inequality. Technological advancement has meant some individuals are engaged in very high-skilled and high-wage employment. However, immigration and growing international competition mean unskilled workers have seen their wages come under increasing pressure, resulting in many individuals being at the bottom of the income distribution because of low pay. The large number of individuals in part-time or temporary employment is causing further income inequality. Unemployment is also a cause of income inequality, particularly for young people as youth unemployment is particularly high.
- **Ownership of assets** — inheritance is a cause of wealth inequality as it enables assets to be passed on to future generations within a family, allowing for the accumulation of wealth over time. Wealth inequality has increased in recent decades as a result of the significant rise in house prices, creating a large gap between the wealth of those who own property and those who are in rented or social housing.
- **Demographic change** — increased life expectancy and a declining birth rate mean the population is ageing. This is creating rising income inequality as a greater proportion of the population is reliant on the state pension.

Exam tip

Wealth inequality is a major cause of income inequality, as assets can be invested to earn an income. For example, individuals who inherit property are able to rent out that property and earn a considerable income from it.

Government policy

The government attempts to reduce income inequality using the tax and benefits system.

Taxes

Direct taxes (taxes on income) are progressive, taking a higher proportion of income from those on high incomes than those on low incomes. In the UK the tax-free personal allowance stood at £10,800 in 2016, meaning all individuals earning less than £10,800 per annum paid no income tax at all. The marginal tax rate increases as income increases, from the basic rate of 20% to the higher rate of 40% to the additional rate of 45% charged on all income earned above £150,000 per annum. Such a tax system helps to reduce income inequality by significantly reducing the income of those at the top of the distribution and incentivising those at the bottom of the distribution to work more hours knowing they do not have to pay any income tax on extra income earned providing their total income is below £10,800.

Benefits

Means-tested benefits are allocated to individuals according to their financial need. They include benefits such as Jobseeker's Allowance, housing benefit and tax credits. These help to increase the income of those at the bottom of the income distribution and do nothing to the income of those at the top of the income distribution (as they are not eligible to receive these benefits).

The combined effect of progressive taxes and means-tested benefits can be illustrated in Figure 4, with government intervention having the effect of shifting the Lorenz curve closer to the line of equality and in doing so making the distribution of income more equal.

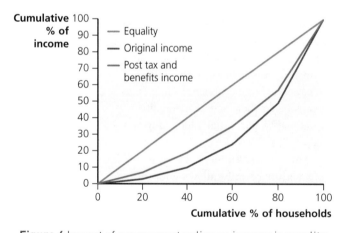

Figure 4 Impact of government policy on income inequality

Evaluating government policies

There are a number of reasons why the tax and benefits system may not achieve the redistribution it initially appears to. First, while direct taxes are progressive, indirect taxes (taxes on spending) tend to be regressive, taking a higher proportion of income from those on low income than those on high income. Goods on which VAT and excise duties are charged tend to take up a higher proportion of income of those on low incomes and therefore serve to increase inequality in the distribution of income.

Knowledge check 5

In addition to income tax, state at least two other types of direct taxes.

Moreover, while means-tested benefits can help to prevent individuals from suffering from absolute poverty, they can create a poverty trap which causes them to suffer relative poverty in the long term. A generous benefits system disincentivises individuals from seeking employment, particularly as they know they will lose their entitlement to such benefits once they start earning an income. While this incentives effect can be overcome with the use of universal benefits which are paid to people regardless of their income, such as the Winter Fuel Allowance, such benefits do not improve the distribution of income as they go to individuals of all income levels.

In the long run, improving the availability of education and training is clearly the best way to improve the distribution of income, as it enables those out of work to find employment and those in low-paid work to increase their earnings potential. However, such policies are not only expensive and involve a time-lag but are difficult to get right, as they rely on the right type of education being provided to genuinely enhance productivity and they require individuals to actually take advantage of this education.

Summary

After studying the topic of *Economic policy objectives and indicators of macroeconomic performance* you should be able to:

- Explain what is meant by economic development.
- Understand how economic development can be measured by GNI per capita, HDI and GPI and evaluate the relative merits of these measures.
- Evaluate the relationship between economic growth and economic development/happiness.
- Evaluate how ODA and trade can promote economic growth and development.
- Explain the role of international organisations such as the IMF, World Bank and WTO in promoting economic growth and development.

- Distinguish between income and wealth inequality.
- Explain and graphically illustrate the different measures of income inequality, including the Lorenz curve and the Gini coefficient.
- Understand what is meant by absolute and relative poverty and explain the causes of poverty and inequality.
- Evaluate the effectiveness of government policies designed to reduce poverty and inequality.

Aggregate demand and aggregate supply

Approaches to macroeconomic equilibrium

Figure 5 illustrates how short-run macroeconomic equilibrium can be reached. Suppose there is an increase in aggregate demand from AD_0 to AD_1. This would initially cause an increase in real output from Y_0 to Y_1. However, the rise in the price level from P_0 to P_1 that this causes is likely to result in further adjustments. As the price level increases, workers may start to demand higher wages to protect their real incomes, while firms may start to be charged higher prices for their inputs. This will raise costs of production for firms, shifting the short-run AS curve in from SAS_0 to SAS_1. This results in the price level rising further to P_2 and real output returning to Y_2.

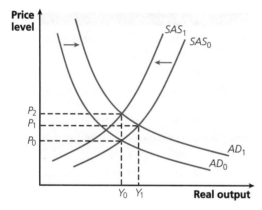

Figure 5 Short-run macroeconomic equilibrium

The extent to which changes in aggregate demand are able to have an impact upon real output is one of the biggest debates that exists in economics. We will now consider the different approaches put forward by economists.

Neoclassical school of thought

The classical and neoclassical school of thought (sometimes referred to as the monetarist approach) puts forward an argument that the economy will rapidly converge to an equilibrium output referred to as the natural rate of output. As illustrated in Figure 6, the long-run aggregate supply curve is vertical in this model, meaning changes in aggregate demand have no impact on real output, as the price level will simply adjust instantaneously to restore equilibrium.

In this model output is always at the natural rate, meaning there is no such thing as disequilibrium unemployment — there is a constant natural rate of unemployment.

Keynesian school of thought

Following years of consistently high unemployment and negative economic growth in the Great Depression, Keynesian economics became an increasingly popular approach to understanding the workings of the macroeconomy. Keynes argued that there

Exam tip

Neoclassical economic theory dictates that the only government policies able to influence the macroeconomic equilibrium are those that affect aggregate supply; demand-side policies will have no impact.

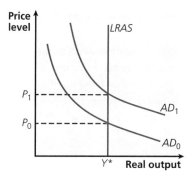

Figure 6 Neoclassical long-run AS

would in fact be a range of outputs over which the aggregate supply curve would be upward sloping, explaining the possibility of employment settling at a level below full employment due to insufficient aggregate demand, such as output level Y_0 in Figure 7.

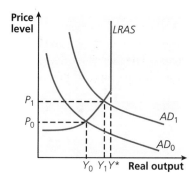

Figure 7 Keynesian long-run AS

Modelling aggregate supply in this way makes a case for government intervention in the economy, as policies designed to stimulate aggregate demand can achieve economic growth by causing an extension along the aggregate supply curve, as illustrated by the growth which occurs from Y_0 to Y_1. This increase in output will increase the derived demand for labour and therefore also contribute towards reduced unemployment.

Keynes proposed that had such policies been adopted during the Great Depression, rather than working on the flawed assumption that the economy would return to equilibrium without intervention, economic recovery could have occurred much more quickly.

Austrian school of thought

The Austrian school of economics points to the failure of traditional economic models to predict and explain what we observe as evidence of the need to embrace the subjective decision making undertaken by individuals based on their own beliefs to be able to explain micro and macroeconomic phenomena. This approach, which is sometimes referred to as methodological individualism because of its focus on individual choice, differs dramatically from other schools of economic thought, which focus on aggregate variables and equilibrium analysis.

Exam tip

Notice that Keynes agreed with classical economic theory about the slope of the aggregate supply curve once full capacity has been reached — at this point it becomes vertical and the only way to increase output is by increasing the quality or quantity of factors of production to expand the productive capacity of the economy.

Austrian economics has made a number of important contributions to economic thought, including:

- **Price determination** — prices are determined by subjective factors such as an individual's preference as to whether or not to buy a particular good. The classical concepts of supply and demand are really based on subjective value judgements — demand is based on individual preference and supply is based on subjective views taken by firms on the value of alternative uses of scarce resources, which is included within costs of production.
- **Interest rate determination** — interest rates are primarily determined by the subjective decision of individuals over whether to spend money now or in the future.

The Phillips curve

In 1958 economist Bill Phillips used empirical data and economic theory to demonstrate the existence of an inverse relationship between unemployment and inflation. He argued that as demand for labour increases and unemployment falls, this puts upward pressure on wage rates as there is more competition for labour. This raises a firm's costs of production, which then get passed onto consumers in the form of higher prices, causing the rate of inflation to increase. The idea of a trade-off between unemployment and inflation is summarised by the Phillips curve in Figure 8.

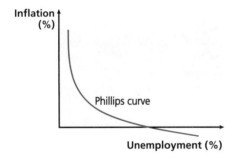

Figure 8 The Phillips curve

The Phillips curve provided evidence that it was possible for the government to manipulate the economy before general elections in order to increase its popularity. Given that in the short run the electorate is more concerned by unemployment than inflation, the Phillips curve suggested that through expansionary policy it was possible for the government to reduce the rate of unemployment in the short run at the cost of higher inflation, which could be dealt with by implementing contractionary policy after winning the election.

However, the **stagflation** experienced in the 1970s started to bring into question the validity of the relationship exposed by Phillips.

Stagflation A situation in which both unemployment and inflation are high at the same time.

Expectations-augmented Phillips curve

In seeking an explanation to stagflation, economists proposed that the Phillips curve may in fact shift over time. It was argued that when entering wage negotiations employees are concerned not by the current rate of inflation but by their expectations of inflation in the future, as their wage rates need to increase by at least the expected future rate of inflation in order for real wages to remain constant. This suggests that changes in inflation expectations can cause the Phillips curve to shift, as illustrated in Figure 9.

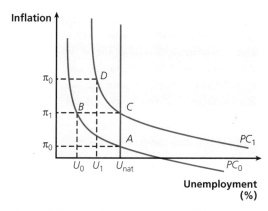

Figure 9 Expectations-augmented Phillips curve

Suppose the economy was initially operating at point A, with unemployment at the natural rate U_{nat} and inflation at π_0. If the government attempted to reduce the unemployment rate to U_0 by allowing the rate of inflation to increase to π_1 this would move the economy to point B. However, employees would observe this higher rate of inflation and adjust their expectations accordingly, causing them to bargain for higher wages and shifting the Phillips curve out to PC_1. At the current rate of inflation of π_1 the economy would reach equilibrium at point C, with unemployment returning to the natural rate of U_{nat}.

This explains why the natural rate of unemployment is sometimes known as the non-accelerating inflation rate of unemployment (NAIRU), as it is the rate of unemployment consistent with a constant rate of inflation. Any attempt to reduce the level of unemployment below the NAIRU will cause the Phillips curve to shift and result in a higher level of inflation.

Neoclassical economists argue that the government will be unable to reduce unemployment below the NAIRU to meet its political objectives, even in the short run, because economic agents will recognise what it is attempting to do and will adjust their expectations instantaneously, meaning any attempt to reduce unemployment will simply result in higher inflation. This suggests the long-run Phillips curve is in fact vertical at the natural rate of unemployment, as shown in Figure 10.

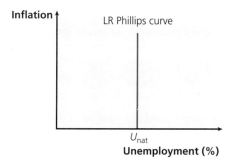

Figure 10 Long-run Phillips curve

Knowledge check 6

If the economy was operating at point C, what would the government need to do in order to reduce the rate of inflation back to π_0?

The economic cycle

Stages of the economic cycle

The economic cycle can be used to illustrate the way in which GDP fluctuates throughout time around an upward trend. The **trend rate of growth** is determined by the growth in the productivity capacity of the economy over time. Because of ongoing technological advancement and the fact that labour productivity tends to increase over time, long-run aggregate supply is thought to increase year on year, producing a trend rate of growth of approximately 2.5%.

Figure 11 illustrates the model of the economic cycle. The stages can be explained as follows:

- **A** — the economy is entering a period of recession, where real GDP is falling.
- **B** — represents the trough in the economy cycle where the difference between potential (trend) and actual GDP is greatest. GDP stops falling and begins to rise again after this point.
- **C** — the recovery phase where actual GDP is growing but is still below trend GDP.
- **D** — the economy begins to boom, with real GDP growing more rapidly than its trend value.
- **E** — the rate of growth begins to slow down, with real output increasing but at a slower rate.
- **F** — represents the peak in the economic cycle where the difference between actual and potential GDP is at its greatest. GDP stops rising and begins to fall after this point, with the economic cycle starting over again.

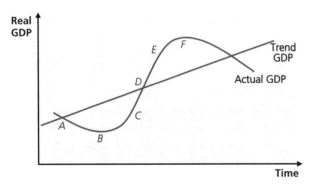

Figure 11 The economic cycle

The economic cycle can be used to illustrate the important distinction between short-run and long-run growth:

- **Short-run growth** — increase in real GDP caused by employing existing unemployed factors of production, as represented by the movement from *B* to *C* in the economic cycle.
- **Long-run growth** — an increase in the productive capacity of the economy, represented by an outward shift in the aggregate supply curve and caused by an increase in the quantity or quality of factors of production. This is illustrated by the upward-sloping trend GDP line on the economic cycle diagram.

> **Trend rate of growth**
> Average sustainable rate of economic growth over a period of time that is consistent with low inflation.

Output gaps

Figure 11 demonstrates that actual GDP may be above or below trend GDP. This difference is known as the output gap, which can be calculated as follows:

    output gap = actual GDP – potential GDP

A negative output gap occurs when actual GDP is below potential GDP. This can be illustrated on both an *AD/AS* and a *PPF* diagram, as shown in Figure 12.

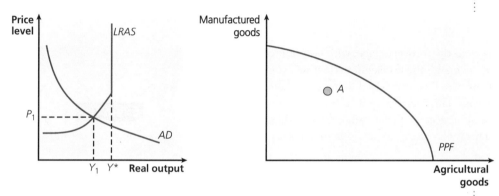

Figure 12 Negative output gap

In these circumstances the economy is not producing to its productive potential as there are unemployed factors of production, meaning policy makers have the incentive to stimulate the economy through expansionary demand-side policies.

A positive output gap occurs when actual GDP exceeds potential GDP. This is shown by the economy operating at point *A* in Figure 13.

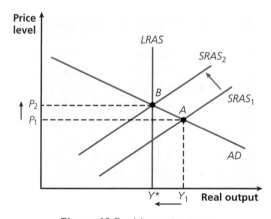

Figure 13 Positive output gap

In this situation the economy is effectively producing beyond its long-run productive capacity. This can be achieved in the short run by some resources being employed beyond their normal capacity — an example being employing labour to work overtime. In the long run, though, this will lead to firms' costs of production rising, as they are competing for increasingly scarce resources, causing the short-run aggregate supply curve to shift to the left from $SRAS_1$ to $SRAS_2$. This will cause real GDP to return to trend GDP at Y^*.

> **Knowledge check 7**
>
> Using an *AD/AS* diagram, explain the impact of expansionary demand-side policies when there is a negative output gap.

The accelerator

The accelerator builds on the concept of the multiplier covered in *Student Guide 2* and concerns investment. There are two motivations for firms to undertake investment:

■ To replace depreciating capital (investment is needed to replace worn-out capital to enable production to continue at current levels).

■ To expand capacity (investment is needed to add to the capital stock to be able to produce more output, which firms will be incentivised to do when they are anticipating an increase in future demand).

When the economic cycle is in the recovery stage, with output increasing as a result of an increase in aggregate demand, the accelerator effect will start operating. As demand has increased, firms will be incentivised to increase their levels of investment to expand productive capacity. This increase in investment will enact a multiplier effect, causing an additional increase in firms' demand and a subsequent further increase in investment. This fuels the economic cycle into a boom.

When output begins to fall, firms experience a fall in demand and as a consequence cut back on investment, undertaking no investment to expand their capacity and potentially not even replacing depreciating capital (as at lower levels of demand they do not need the same productive capacity). This fall in investment will cause a negative multiplier effect, which will result in investment falling still further. This fuels the economic cycle into a recession.

Exam tip

The way the multiplier and the accelerator interact is part of what causes such significant fluctuations in output over the course of the economic cycle.

Summary

After studying the topic of *Aggregate demand and aggregate supply* you should be able to:

■ Understand the Keynesian, neoclassical and Austrian schools of thought and evaluate the implications of these different approaches for policy makers.

■ Explain what is meant by the Phillips curve and the natural rate of unemployment.

■ Explain why the Phillips curve may be vertical in the long run and why the natural rate of unemployment can be referred to as the non-accelerating inflation rate of unemployment (NAIRU).

■ Evaluate the implications of the Phillips curve for policy makers.

■ Explain the different stages of the economic cycle.

■ Understand what is meant by the trend rate of growth and how it is determined.

■ Explain the concept of positive and negative output gaps using *AD/AS* and *PPF* diagrams and evaluate the impact of output gaps on macroeconomic policy.

■ Explain the economic cycle using the multiplier–accelerator model.

The application of policy instruments

Approaches to macroeconomic policy

Debates in macroeconomic thinking

Economists do not agree on how the macroeconomy works. This is largely because of the different assumptions they make on the following issues:

- **The elasticity of aggregate supply** — neoclassical economists assume that the long-run aggregate supply curve is vertical at the natural rate of output and employment, as the macroeconomy rapidly adjusts to shocks to return to the long-run equilibrium. This approach suggests that there will never be an output gap and, therefore, that there is no role for the government to play in the macroeconomy, except in pursuing supply-side policies to support the expansion in the productive capacity over time. Keynesians, however, argue that there is a range of levels of output for which long-run aggregate supply is upward sloping, meaning that the economy can be caught at an equilibrium level of output below full capacity. This implies government policy is important in manipulating the level of aggregate demand to achieve a desired level of output.

- **The extent to which prices and wages are flexible** — the neoclassical belief that the long-run aggregate supply curve is vertical is based on the assumption that markets can adjust instantaneously. In product markets this implies that prices are fully flexible, while in labour markets wages are equally flexible. Keynesians argue that there is strong evidence to suggest that such variables are not flexible, particularly wages. They point to wages being 'sticky' downwards. When demand for a firm's product falls, the demand for labour falls. In a flexible labour market wages should adjust downwards to enable the labour market to return to equilibrium. However, workers are likely to resist nominal wage cuts, particularly when supported by union intervention. This means there is likely to be disequilibrium unemployment and again implies a role for the government.

- **The role of expectations** — neoclassical economists assume that individuals rapidly reach accurate expectations about the future, allowing equilibrium at the natural rate of output and employment to be sustained. This is evidenced by their conclusion of the long-run Phillips curve being vertical, which is based on the belief that economic agents will hold accurate expectations about future inflation rates. However, if expectations are in fact slow to adjust, this suggests that in the short run it could be possible for the government to reduce the level of unemployment below the natural rate by allowing inflation to increase. Expectations are also important in explaining investment decisions, with firms thought unlikely to undertake investment when they are uncertain about the economic climate because of fluctuating inflation. This provides a strong argument for governments pursuing low and stable inflation in order to improve confidence and incentivise investment.

Exam tip

The idea of nominal wages being 'sticky' downwards provides an argument for the government targeting a positive inflation rate, as it gives firms real wage flexibility despite the existence of nominal wage rigidity by allowing them to increase nominal wages by less than the rate of inflation.

Policy approaches over time

The Great Depression

Classical economics represented mainstream economic thought at the time of the Great Depression in the 1930s. When unemployment rose dramatically following the 1929 Wall Street Crash, policy makers believed the market would automatically adjust without intervention to reach equilibrium, and that all that was needed was for wages and prices to fall. However, despite a period of falling prices and wages, international competitiveness did not improve and unemployment remained high, resulting in a **depression** occurring in the economy.

Depression A long and severe recession.

The Keynesian revolution

The failure of classical economics in dealing with the Great Depression resulted in economists seeking new ways to model the macroeconomy. This was led by Keynes, who believed that the depression could have ended more quickly if the government had engaged in active demand management.

Keynes was a crucial figure at the Bretton Woods conference in 1946, which set the rules for international trade in the post-war era. This involved the construction of a fixed exchange rate system which became known as the Dollar Standard, where all currencies were fixed against the US dollar. This had significant implications for macroeconomic policy. With monetary policy unable to be used for domestic purposes in order for it to be used to support the fixed exchange rate, this increased the role of fiscal policy in the management of the macroeconomy. The Keynesian approach of smoothing out the economic cycle by using discretionary fiscal policy became popular and initially led to a so-called 'golden era' in the 1950s and 1960s, with unemployment and inflation both relatively low.

However, underlying economic instability existed throughout the period in the form of a stop–go cycle. When the economy began to boom, rising real incomes led to rising demand for imports, forcing the government to implement contractionary monetary policy to maintain the exchange rate. In doing so, this slowed the rate of economic growth.

By the early 1970s the Dollar Standard had been abandoned as a result of exchange rate problems caused by high inflation in the USA due to its involvement in the Vietnam War. This opened up the potential for monetary policy to once again be used to achieve domestic macroeconomic policy objectives.

The monetarist counter-revolution

The stagflation that occurred in the 1970s provided evidence that Keynesian economics was not working and led to the rise of Friedman's monetarist approach, which argued for the return of classical economic thinking. When in 1976 the UK government had to borrow from the IMF to deal with a balance of payments crisis, one of the conditions attached to the loan was targeting the growth in money supply to prevent inflation spiralling out of control.

This represented the start of a new era in macroeconomic policy, with monetary policy once more becoming the main instrument used by the government. Price stability was considered the primary purpose of policy, as achieving this would enable

Exam tip

Providing some historical context in your exam answers will impress the examiner. When evaluating the effectiveness of policy you should recognise the assumptions you are making and explain how the outcome would be different if approached from a Keynesian/neoclassical perspective.

markets to fulfil their role in allocating resources and result in increased investment by firms, which had greater confidence in the economic climate when prices were not fluctuating. The only role played by the government in stimulating the economy was through supply-side policy, with a return to the belief that the role of the government was to expand the productive capacity of the economy by doing things such as stimulating enterprise.

The 2007–8 financial crisis and its aftermath

The 2008 global financial crisis resulted in the UK economy experiencing the most severe recession since the Great Depression. The crisis highlighted the interdependence and risk of financial **contagion**, which exists in today's globalised world, and once again brought into question the notion of markets being left to their own devices, with financial deregulation being heavily blamed for causing the problems in the financial sector.

Contagion The spread of either economic booms or crises across geographic areas.

The aftermath of the financial crisis also saw the notion of price stability being the primary macroeconomic objective come under question. Despite successive periods of above-target inflation, interest rates remained at a record low of 0.5% as the Bank of England was seen to prioritise the economic recovery. Keynesian ideas of demand-side management also regained popularity, with a range of expansionary fiscal policies such as reducing VAT introduced in an attempt to stimulate the economy.

The post-crisis period has been characterised by a debate over how the government should respond to rising national debt. Governments across the world have taken different approaches to this, with some adopting a traditional Keynesian standpoint of running expansionary fiscal policy in an attempt to generate the economic growth needed to reduce debt in the long term, while others have adopted contractionary 'austerity' policies considered essential in providing the macroeconomic credibility needed for investment. The debate is ongoing as economists continue to formulate new methods of modelling the macroeconomy in light of the financial crisis.

Summary

After studying the topic of *The application of policy instruments* you should be able to:

■ Understand the debates that exist in macroeconomic thinking, comparing Keynesian and neoclassical approaches with the key issues of the flexibility of prices, the elasticity of aggregate supply and the role of expectations.

■ Evaluate how different approaches to macroeconomic thinking impact upon the effectiveness of particular macroeconomic policies.

■ Explain how approaches to macroeconomic policy have changed over time, with reference to the Great Depression, 1970s' Keynesian demand management, 1980s' monetarism and the 2007–8 financial crisis and its aftermath.

◼ The global context

Globalisation

Causes of globalisation

Globalisation is the process by which the world's economies are becoming ever more closely integrated. It is characterised by rising global trade and the increased mobility of factors of production between countries. There are a number of factors that explain the rise of globalisation:

- **Advances in technology of transport and communication** — it has become easier and cheaper for firms to sell and produce products across the world.
- **Reduction in trade barriers** — declining protectionism caused by the free trade movement has enabled foreign firms to compete with domestic firms in many countries.
- **Deregulation of financial markets** — this has enabled financial markets across the world to become more closely integrated, leading to huge increases in foreign direct investment.

External shocks

While globalisation has clearly contributed to an increase in world output by enabling countries to develop and exploit their comparative advantage, closer integration between nations has left countries more vulnerable to external shocks.

One example of this is the problems fluctuating oil prices can cause for many economies, with sudden changes causing widespread disruption. In the late 2000s, rising global demand coupled with supply-side constraints caused a spike in the oil price and resulted in significant balance of payments problems for net importers of oil.

The most significant recent example of the danger posed by the prospect of external shocks is of course the financial contagion which occurred following the 2007–8 global financial crisis. When individuals began defaulting on their debt caused by sub-prime lending in the USA, this led to a credit crunch which quickly resulted in a tightening on lending around the world, plunging a number of countries into recession and requiring coordinated action on cutting interest rates to improve the flow of credit. The problems the default caused to many eurozone nations were particularly severe, with Ireland, Greece and Portugal all requiring bail-outs to avoid defaulting on their national debt repayments.

Foreign direct investment

One of the most significant features of globalisation has been the rapid increase in foreign direct investment (FDI). There are three primary factors that have motivated multinational corporations (MNCs) to increase their level of foreign direct investment:

- **Market seeking** — MNCs are attracted by selling their products across the world as producing for a larger market may enable them to benefit from economies of scale and increase their revenue. One way to access a new market is to produce

Exam tip

It is not inevitable that a financial crisis in one country will spread around the world. The Asian crisis which occurred in the late 1990s caused largely by Thailand having made inefficient use of foreign direct investment is a good example of a crisis that did not spread beyond the neighbouring countries of Indonesia, Malaysia, the Philippines and South Korea, despite the links those economies had with Western countries.

within the market, which may be desirable as it reduces transportation costs and may enable the firm to avoid trade barriers. This has been a significant factor explaining the rise of FDI in China, where MNCs have been desperate to gain access to this huge and increasingly affluent market. The same can be said of FDI in the EU, which has seen substantial inward flows of investment by firms seeking access to the single market.

- **Resource seeking** — MNCs may want to take advantage of a natural resource within a country, such as oil, or produce there because it enables them to access cheap or particularly skilled labour.
- **Efficiency seeking** — an MNC might relocate a particular part of its production process to another country because it knows this will increase the efficiency of production, lowering costs and increasing profits.

FDI is generally considered to be of significant benefit to the recipient country. Such investment tends to bring with it jobs for domestic workers, reducing unemployment and raising tax revenue both through higher income tax receipts and taxes on the profits of MNCs operating within the country.

One of the most valuable benefits derived from FDI is the new capital and technology MNCs often bring to a country, which in the long run can cause spillover effects by improving the productivity of domestic firms, which learn from the MNCs and benefit from being able to employ a more skilled workforce. Most economists view these advantages as outweighing the potential risk that FDI might lead to domestic firms being competed out of their own markets.

LDCs and emerging economies

While FDI makes an important contribution to many developed economies, its impact has perhaps been greatest on the world's least developed countries (LDCs) emerging economies. There exists much debate over whether FDI has contributed to or hindered economic development in these nations — the arguments on each side are summarised in Table 2 on page 28.

Despite the significant amount of investment which has flowed into developing countries, the fact that LDCs have generally struggled to catch up with developed countries perhaps demonstrates the limitations of FDI in promoting economic development.

A group of countries which has bucked this trend is the BRIC nations, comprised of Brazil, Russia, India and China. These countries have seen accelerating growth rates and human development and meet regularly, along with South Africa, to form strategy. In 2015 these nations accounted for 20% of global GDP and 40% of the world's population.

China's growth has been particularly impressive, given the size of its population and ability to continue to grow throughout the global financial crisis. In 2014 it overtook the USA to become the world's largest economy. This growth has been based on a policy of export-led growth, with a fixed exchange rate regime enabling Chinese firms to remain internationally price competitive.

Knowledge check 8

Explain what is meant by foreign direct investment.

Exam tip

It is important to understand that the impact of FDI on economic development varies dramatically between nations. Make sure you recognise this in any exam answer and are able to explain what determines the extent to which countries are able to benefit from such investment.

Table 2

Advantages	Disadvantages
A major barrier to development in LDCs is that low income per capita means there is little saving and thus no significant funds for investment. FDI represents a vital injection into the circular flow, providing the funds for investment needed for development to take place.	MNCs are generally considered to be profit maximisers. This may involve them engaging in limit or predatory pricing to drive domestic firms out of business, after which they will be able to act as a monopolist and set prices high and keep output low. This will harm domestic consumers. MNCs may also pollute the environment to keep costs low.
FDI gives countries access to sophisticated capital and technology, overcoming LDCs' limited capacity to produce capital goods and enabling them to move away from an economy dominated by agricultural production.	MNCs may pay above the equilibrium wage rate in order to attract the best workers and maintain a good public image. This could harm local firms, which struggle to attract or hold on to their best workers.
MNCs may provide training and skills to domestic workers, developing human capital and potentially creating entrepreneurial spirit in the LDC. In the long term these more highly skilled individuals may take up jobs with domestic firms or set up their own businesses, contributing to economic growth.	Much of the employment provided by MNCs is likely to be low skilled, with the more highly skilled and managerial roles often filled by expatriate workers.
By providing a large number of jobs in the urban areas in which they set up, MNCs can help overcome the crisis LDCs have faced with rising migration to cities and an inability to find jobs for these people.	MNCs may use production methods which are familiar to them from their developed country of origin. This is likely to be capital intensive, meaning the employment effects may not be as great as first thought. Moreover, they may simply encourage greater migration to already overcrowded cities and further widen rural–urban inequality.
The tax revenues provided by taxing MNCs' profits and the earnings of workers employed by the MNCs enables LDCs to invest in crucial public sector services such as healthcare and education.	The LDC may have to offer MNCs tax concessions to prevent them relocating, reducing potential tax revenues. Moreover, MNCs may engage in illegal transfer pricing, where they set prices for internal transactions within the company, which enables them to pay tax on profits in a country with the lowest corporation tax rate.

The performance of the emerging economies can be seen to have both positive and negative impacts on developed nations. On the one hand, rising incomes in developing nations has provided a larger market for MNCs to sell to, boosting their profits and increasing exports. On the other hand, countries such as China could be seen to have harmed the balance of payments in developed nations because of the ability of Chinese firms to undercut the prices of firms operating in developed economies.

International trade

Terms of trade

A country's terms of trade — calculated by the ratio of export prices to import prices — is crucial in determining its gains from trade.

Inflation means that export and import prices are generally rising over time. However, if import prices are rising more rapidly than export prices in a particular country then its terms of trade are worsening — the country must now export a greater volume of its goods in order to get the same volume of imports.

While a deterioration in the terms of trade is likely to harm the balance of payments, this will not be the case if the volume of exports is increasing sufficiently rapidly. Suppose, for example, the terms of trade worsen by 10% during a period in which the volume of exports increases by 15%. The fall in the relative value of exports will be offset by the rise in the volume of exports and should, *ceteris paribus*, result in the balance of payments improving.

Terms of trade in LDCs

The fact that LDCs tend to specialise in the exporting of primary products causes significant problems for their terms of trade:

- **Short-run volatility caused by price volatility** — prices are particularly volatile for primary sector products. Agricultural products tend to have relatively stable and inelastic demand but volatile supply, as the supply of agricultural goods is heavily dependent on the climate and season. Raw materials, meanwhile, have relatively stable and inelastic supply but volatile demand, as the demand for raw materials fluctuates with the economic cycle in developed countries, which are the primary users of raw materials. In both cases this leads to significant price volatility of exports, which causes the terms of trade to fluctuate over time. Such instability in export revenue can be damaging for developing nations, which rely on international trade as a path to development.

- **Long-run deterioration in terms of trade** — the Prebisch–Singer hypothesis argues that the terms of trade of primary product-based economies deteriorates over time. This is because the demand for primary sector products is relatively income inelastic — as incomes increase, food expenditure, for example, falls as a proportion of disposable income, meaning as the world economy grows, there is little increase in demand. Moreover, supply for primary sector products tends to increase over time because technological developments improve the efficiency of production. The result is that the price of exports for developing nations is on a downward trend. The reverse is true for imports of secondary and tertiary sector products, which are rising in price over time because of increased demand resulting from the income-elastic nature of demand for such products. With the price of exports falling and the price of imports rising, this means the terms of trade of many developing nations are declining each year.

Both of these issues mean that developing countries often struggle to enjoy significant gains from trade because of their reliance on primary sector production. This provides strong justification as to why diversifying the economy is so important in enabling LDCs to develop.

Pattern of comparative advantage

Declining terms of trade for primary producers mean that in many ways developing countries have found themselves trapped by their pattern of comparative advantage rather than in a position to be able to exploit it. This is not an easy problem to overcome, as it is only the comparative advantage they enjoy in the production of primary products over developed nations that enables them to engage in international trade in the first place.

Knowledge check 9

If between 2006 and 2016 the price index of exports has increased by 22% and the price index of imports has increased by 14%, what has happened to the terms of trade? Assume that the price indexes for imports and exports are based on 2006 = 100.

Exam tip

Countries in South East Asia have proved it is possible to change the structure of an economy over time, moving away from a reliance on primary sector production to manufacturing, which has partly been achieved by investing in appropriate infrastructure and giving high-quality technical training to the workforce to improve their skills in this area.

The proportion of GDP accounted for by international trade varies significantly between countries. The importance of trade fundamentally depends upon whether a country has the resources needed to trade — it needs to produce the sorts of goods that other countries want to buy in order to attract export demand. Moreover, it depends upon policy makers' attitude to international trade. While governments in South East Asia have pursued policies of export-led growth, countries such as India have historically been less keen to engage in trade and have subsequently created frameworks that have limited the expansion of trade.

Heckscher–Ohlin theory

The Heckscher–Ohlin theory proposes that a country's comparative advantage will depend on its relative endowments of factors of production, with countries specialising in the production of goods which intensively utilise the factors of production of which they have an abundant supply. For example, a country which has an abundant supply of capital but a labour shortage will specialise in the production of goods that require little labour but lots of capital.

There is strong empirical evidence to support this theory as explaining patterns of trade. LDCs rich in natural resources, a plentiful supply of labour but lacking in capital often specialise in labour- or land-intensive production, while developed nations such as the UK and the USA specialise in capital-intensive activity such as financial services or manufacturing. Over time, as South East Asian economies have developed comparative advantage in manufacturing, Western economies have increasingly moved towards tertiary sector production.

It is clearly tempting for countries to rely on natural comparative advantage to dictate international trade. However, the evolution of terms of trade over time means that developing nations might need to seek to alter the pattern of their comparative advantage in order to catch up with developed nations.

Trade policies and negotiations

Protectionism

We have already seen a number of reasons why international trade can present problems for a country, ranging from domestic firms being outcompeted by foreign multinational corporations to balance of payments deficits resulting from declining terms of trade over time. In order to counter these and other problems a country may choose to engage in protectionism, defined as any attempt to impose restrictions on the trade in goods and services. The different protectionist policies available to a government are detailed below.

Tariffs

A tariff is a tax imposed on imports. The impact of imposing a tariff on a good can be seen in Figure 14. D represents the domestic demand for the product and S_{dom} represents the domestic supply.

Knowledge check 10

In order to overcome the problems explained by the Prebisch–Singer hypothesis, explain why a country may want to employ protectionist measures to protect newly developing sectors in an economy.

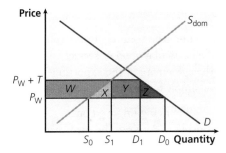

Figure 14 The effects of a tariff

Let us first consider the situation before the tariff was imposed. Domestic consumers are able to import the good from foreign producers at a price of P_w. We assume global supply is perfectly elastic because the domestic country is too small to influence the world price. At a price of P_w, D_0 units of the good are demanded by consumers. S_0 units will be supplied by domestic firms and the remaining $(D_0 - S_0)$ units are imports supplied by foreign firms.

In order to protect domestic firms the government may impose a tariff of T on foreign producers. This will raise the price at which consumers can purchase the good to $Pw + T$. This has a number of effects on the market:

- Domestic firms will sell more — domestic production increases from S_0 to S_1. By being able to sell at a higher price producers gain additional producer surplus equal to area W.
- Imports fall dramatically to $(D_1 - S_1)$. The government raises tax revenue from the tariff on these units of output equal to area Y.
- At a higher price demand for the product falls from D_0 to D_1. This higher price has a negative impact on consumers, with consumer surplus falling by $W + X + Y + Z$.

Clearly, some of the consumer surplus lost has been redistributed to domestic firms (W) and the government (Y). But there is also a deadweight loss, equal to area $X + Y$. Society is therefore worse off as a result of the tariff being imposed, as the government is essentially subsidising inefficient domestic producers.

While such a policy should protect jobs and improve the balance of payments, this comes at a cost. Consumers suffer from consuming less output at higher prices and producers may develop X-inefficiency as a result of being kept artificially competitive, which in the long run could damage their ability to compete in the global market. However, if the tariff is designed as a short-term measure to protect infant industries to enable a developing country to adopt a new comparative advantage and in doing so reduce its reliance on primary sector production, it could perhaps be justified to enable domestic firms to achieve international competitiveness in the long run in this sector.

The effectiveness of such a policy crucially depends on the reaction of other nations. There is evidence that other countries tend to retaliate when tariffs are imposed on their producers. This will result in the global gains from trade being reduced as comparative advantage will not be able to be fully exploited across the world.

Exam tip

Although a tariff may initially appear to be a bad idea it is important to consider the context in which it is being imposed, using the material on the declining terms of trade many LDCs are experiencing to justify why temporarily protecting infant industries may be advantageous.

Quotas and non-tariff barriers

Quotas are an alternative protectionist policy designed to limit the volume of imports by placing a specific limit on the quantity of imports of a particular good or service allowed from a country. This can be done either with the agreement of the exporting country through **voluntary export restraints** (VERs) or simply be imposed upon them.

Voluntary export restraint Where a country agrees to limit its exports to another country to a given quantity.

Figure 15 illustrates the impact of a quota. Prior to the quota being imposed on Country A, the competitive equilibrium is the same as explained before the tariff was imposed in Figure 14 — domestic production takes place at S_0, $(D_0 - S_0)$ units of the good are imported from Country A and the price is at P_a. It is assumed that Country A produces the good on a large enough scale for supply to be perfectly elastic at P_a.

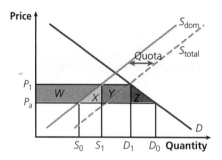

Figure 15 The effects of a quota

When a quota is imposed there is no longer an infinite supply of the good from Country A. Supply to the domestic market is now represented by S_{total}, comprised of domestic supply plus the total amount of imports permitted into the country. The result is that the price increases to P_1. There are a number of implications of imposing a quota:

- Domestic producers sell more — S_1 rather than S_0 — and gain a producer surplus of area W by being able to sell at a higher price.
- Those foreign producers that are still importing gain a producer surplus equal to area Y, as they are able to sell their goods at a higher price than previously.
- Consumers lose out from consuming less and having to pay higher prices, meaning a loss of consumer surplus of $W + X + Y + Z$.

While some of the lost consumer surplus has been redistributed to domestic (W) and foreign (Y) firms, there is overall a net welfare loss to society of $X + Z$. As with a tariff, while the end result might benefit domestic producers in the short term, there is a concern that restricting the amount of competition they face could in the long term lead to X-inefficiency. There is also a risk that other countries will retaliate by imposing quotas of their own, which could harm domestic firms in industries where the country enjoys a comparative advantage.

As part of the global free trade movement a number of quotas have been removed around the world. One such example of this is the removal of a series of quotas imposed by the USA to limit the volume of imports of textiles from China. There exists significant debate over the relative merits of removing such quotas. It is certainly good for textiles producers in China, who find themselves with a larger market to sell to, and will benefit consumers in the USA, who are able to purchase textiles at lower prices. The impact on workers in the USA is more uncertain — on the one hand there is a risk of them suffering unemployment as domestic textiles firms are outcompeted, but on the other it frees up workers to be employed in high-productivity sectors. The clear losers are countries such as Sri Lanka and Bangladesh, which previously exported significant volumes of textiles to the USA and now find themselves facing competition from Chinese firms.

Trade can also be limited by the imposition of a range of non-tariff barriers. These are policies comprised of rules and regulations designed to control the standard of products that legally can be sold within a country. This can stop foreign producers importing their goods and can advantage domestic producers, who are often more able to comply with the specific quality standards imposed as the government imposing them has set such standards with the protection of domestic firms in mind.

Economic integration

The objective of economic integration is to enable trading partners to take advantage of the potential gains from international trade by removing or reducing barriers to trade so that countries can engage in greater specialisation and exploit their comparative advantage. Regional trade agreements can take a number of forms, representing different stages of economic integration.

Free trade areas

A free trade area is defined as a group of countries that agrees to remove tariffs, quotas and other restrictions on trade between member countries but has no agreement on a common barrier against non-members. Members are therefore free to impose their own patterns of tariffs and quotas on non-members.

There are a number of examples of free trade areas in operation around the world:
- **EFTA** (European Free Trade Association) — initially a free trade area for European countries which did not want to or were unable to join the European Economic Community (now the European Union). The UK remained a member of EFTA before joining the EU in 1973. EFTA is now comprised of Iceland, Liechtenstein, Norway and Switzerland.
- **ASEAN** (Association of South East Asian Nations) — formed in 1967 and includes countries such as Indonesia, Malaysia and Vietnam.
- **NAFTA** (North American Free Trade Association) — formed in 1994 and covers the USA, Canada and Mexico. By 2008 all tariff barriers had been removed between these nations and there had been a subsequent increase in trade and investment as a consequence. However, within the USA there are concerns about job losses which have occurred as a result of the agreement, while Mexico's agricultural sector has been damaged by the competition it has faced from subsidised imports from the USA.

Customs unions

Customs unions represent areas in which there exists free trade between members but also an agreement on a common set of external restrictions, with a common external tariff imposed on non-member states.

The gains from operating within a customs union can be seen in Figure 16, which illustrates the trade creation that occurs when a country joins a customs union.

Knowledge check 11

Why might it be more effective for a country to impose a quota rather than a tariff?

Exam tip

The lack of a common external tariff can be problematic, as non-members will be incentivised to channel imports into the member country with the lowest tariffs and then resell the products within the free trade area to other member countries. This can distort the pattern of trade and create unnecessary transaction costs.

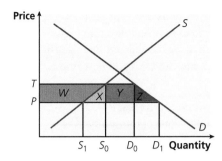

Figure 16 Trade creation

Assume that before joining the customs union a country imposed tariffs on foreign producers which meant there was a perfectly elastic world supply at a price of T. At this price domestic demand was at D_0, which was met by S_0 units of domestic production and $(D_0 - S_0)$ units of imports.

When the country joins the customs union other member states are able to import to the country without tariffs being imposed. Consumers are now able to access the good at a price of P. This has a number of effects:

■ Consumers benefit from consuming more of the good (at D_1) at a lower price, meaning consumer surplus increases by $W + X + Y + Z$.

■ Domestic producers lose out — they now sell only S_1, and at a lower price than before. There is therefore a loss of producer surplus of area W.

■ The government loses out on the tariff revenue of Y it used to earn before imports started coming from a customs union member upon which no tariff was imposed.

Joining a customs union therefore results in some redistribution of welfare away from domestic firms (W) and the government (Y) towards consumers in the form of enhanced consumer surplus. Overall, though, there is a net welfare gain equal to area $X + Z$. This illustrates the gains from trade which occur from countries being able to engage in greater international specialisation and exploit comparative advantage.

While such analysis suggests customs unions have a highly positive impact on a country, the theory of trade diversion suggests that some of these gains are overstated. With a system of common external tariffs in place it may be that the increased trade that takes place between member nations is simply replacing trade that previously took place with non-members. This is illustrated in Figure 17.

> ### Knowledge check 12
>
> Despite the loss in producer surplus of area W illustrated in Figure 16, explain why domestic producers may in fact benefit from being part of a customs union.

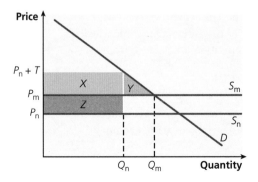

Figure 17 Trade diversion

First consider the situation before a country decides to join a customs union. S_n and S_m represent the supply of a particular good from a non-member and member of the customs union respectively. Before joining the customs union, the country imposed the same tariff on both countries. It would therefore import from Country N, the non-member, as this is the more efficient producer able to supply the good at a price of $P_n + T$ with a tariff imposed (the price including the tariff for Country M would be higher than this). This would result in a quantity of Q_n being imported.

Once the country joins the customs union, no tariffs are imposed on imports from Country M. This incentivises the country to switch from importing from Country N (which still faces a tariff and so can import at a price of $P_n + T$) to Country M, which can import at a price of P_m. Q_m units will be imported. This has a number of effects:

- Consumers benefit from consuming more of the good at a lower price, so consumer surplus increases by $X + Y$.
- The government loses out on the tariff revenue of $X + Z$ that it used to collect.

While some of the government revenue (X) has been redistributed to consumers in the form of lower prices, some of it (Z) is now lost to the economy and represents payment by domestic consumers to foreign producers. Here, it is clear to see that the country gains from being a part of a customs union only if area Y exceeds area Z.

In addition, there are wider disadvantages that can occur from being part of a customs union. Along with the transaction costs involved with administering the union, inequality between regions within the union has the potential to increase. This is because firms may choose to locate near the centre of a customs union in order to minimise transport costs, or alternatively locate in the richest part of the market where demand will be greatest. This means that countries that either have low incomes or are geographically isolated may struggle to enjoy the gains from being part of a customs union.

These disadvantages therefore needed to be weighed up against the potential advantages that can come to consumers in the form of lower prices and the long-run advantages that can come to firms as a result of being exposed to more international competition and having a larger market to sell to within the union.

Common market

A common market represents a step towards full economic integration and occurs when member countries can trade freely in all economic resources, not just goods and services. This means there is free movement of capital and labour. Members are likely to agree on a series of common microeconomic policies, such as rules concerning monopoly power and other anti-competitive practices. It is also likely common markets will have put in place a common public sector procurement policy, so that individual governments do not favour domestic firms when purchasing goods and services.

Monetary union

Monetary union involves the adoption of a single currency, such as the euro. This means member countries share a common exchange rate and monetary policy, with a single central bank such as the European Central Bank (ECB) setting interest rates and regulating the money supply. Once countries have integrated to this level they are no longer able to use monetary policy as a domestic policy tool, which can be problematic when countries are at different stages of the economic cycle.

Exam tip

Trade diversion provides a powerful argument against customs unions, as it essentially encourages trade to be diverted away from more efficient non-members towards less efficient members who are made artificially competitive because they are not charged a tariff. Patterns of trade being altered in this way goes against the theory of comparative advantage.

Knowledge check 13

Explain why a country experiencing a recession which is part of a monetary union may not be able to use monetary policy to stimulate economic growth.

Economic union

Some economists argue that monetary union can operate effectively only when there is full economic union within a country, which would include fiscal union. This would require countries to harmonise tax rates, establish common levels of public sector spending and borrowing and reach agreement over the size of national budget deficits and surpluses. The loss of control this brings to domestic governments means full fiscal union is unpopular in many countries.

The European Union

Founded in 1957 when Belgium, France, Italy, Luxembourg, the Netherlands and West Germany signed the Treaty of Rome, the European Union had by 2016 grown to be one of the world's most prominent examples of regional trade integration, with 28 member states and a total population in excess of 500 million citizens.

The Single European Market

As part of a process towards achieving a single market in 1993, a number of steps were taken, including the removal of border controls and the winding down of non-tariff barriers to trade. There are a number of reasons to explain why the common market was considered an important part of the European project:

- Reduced transaction costs in a free trade area would enable the gains from trade to be fully exploited.
- Operating in a common market provides a larger market for firms to sell to, enabling them to enjoy greater economies of scale and as a result increase the efficiency with which they produce.
- Firms will be forced to eliminate X-inefficiencies in order to survive the more intense competition they will face from firms across the common market.

The Single Currency Area

The establishment of the European Monetary System (EMS) and the Exchange Rate Mechanism (ERM) in 1979 represented the first significant step towards monetary union. Members of the ERM agreed to maintain their exchange rates within a 2.25% symmetric band against the average of all member countries (the European Currency Unit). While 11 realignments of various currencies took place between 1979 and 1987, the conditions for being permitted a realignment became more stringent over time and fewer such adjustments took place as the mechanism became more established. Note that the UK largely remained outside of the ERM except for brief involvement between 1990 and 1992.

In 1989 the Delors Plan set out proposals for monetary union, including plans for the creation of an independent central bank. This was followed in 1993 by the Maastricht Treaty, which as well as providing a range of significant social policies set out the crucial convergence criteria countries needed to meet in order to be invited to join the single currency. The conditions for entry into the euro were as follows:

- **Low and similar inflation rates** — inflation rate could be no more than 1.5% above the average of the three countries in the EMS with the lowest inflation rate. While one of the benefits of a single currency was perceived to be more stable prices, it was thought a country could not reasonably join a monetary union with countries with 1% inflation when their inflation rate was 20%.

> **Exam tip**
>
> The southern European states were initially thought to benefit most from joining the single market because of their differing pattern of comparative advantage from western European economies. The relative labour abundance present in such countries meant they could specialise in labour-intensive production and sell those products across the single market to countries specialising in capital-intensive production.

- **Similar long-term interest rates** — the interest rate could be no more than 2% above the average of the three EMS countries with the lowest rate. Given that financial capital follows high interest rates, relatively similar interest rates were needed to avoid instability in capital flows.
- **Budget deficit to be no greater than 3% of GDP** — this ensured aspiring members had a similar short-term fiscal stance. Vastly different fiscal positions had the potential to undermine monetary union, as member states could be required to make big fiscal transfers to other member states once they shared a currency, as the performance of their economies would be so heavily interlinked.
- **National debt to be no greater than 60% of GDP** — if countries did this it would demonstrate a long-term commitment to sustainable fiscal policy. This was crucial, as admitting a country to the eurozone with an unsustainable level of national debt could cause problems in the future, with foreign investors likely to withdraw not just from the struggling country but from all eurozone nations because of their shared currency.

The final step towards the creation of the single currency was the establishment of the European Economic and Monetary Union (EMU) where exchange rates between participating countries were permanently locked together. In 1999 the ECB began its operations and became responsible for setting common interest rates across the region.

The euro eventually launched in 2002 with 12 member states — Belgium, Germany, Greece, Spain, France, Ireland, Italy, Luxembourg, the Netherlands, Austria, Portugal and Finland. By 2015 they had been joined by Slovenia, Cyprus, Malta, Slovakia, Estonia, Latvia and Lithuania.

There are a number of costs and benefits associated with a single currency area, as shown in Table 3.

Table 3

Benefits	Costs
The reduced transaction costs arising from no longer having to convert one currency to another made trade easier and cheaper, enabling countries to better exploit comparative advantage.	With interest rates set by the ECB, individual member states lost control of monetary policy, making it more difficult to respond to external shocks and therefore potentially accentuating the economic cycle.
Confidence and certainty improved as a result of no longer having to forecast future movements in exchange rates between member countries. This encouraged more foreign investment and gave member states access to cheaper borrowing.	When a country finds itself at a different stage of the economic cycle to another member nation it could find the centralised policies imposed particularly damaging. For example, an interest rate increase designed to curb eurozone-wide inflation could harm a member state which would prefer expansionary monetary policy because it is suffering from a recession.

Economist Paul Krugman has put forward the argument that a single currency is most effective the greater the degree of integration between nations, with the benefits rising and costs falling as the closeness of integration increases. This is illustrated in Figure 18.

Exam tip

One of the problems with the construction of the euro was the lack of enforcement of the convergence criteria. This meant that eurozone members such as Greece, for example, were able to build up a debt to GDP ratio in excess of 100% by 2006, which created significant problems by the time the global financial crisis hit.

Knowledge check 14

Explain what is meant by price transparency and why this is likely to be another advantage of a single currency.

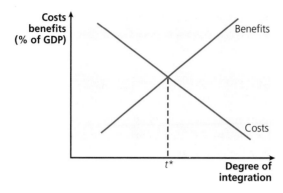

Figure 18 Costs and benefits of a single currency area

Essentially, Krugman argued that countries needed to assess whether they were integrated at least to point t^* before joining a single currency, as such closeness was needed in order to make membership of a single currency worthwhile. Only when the benefits of joining a single currency outweigh the costs can it be considered to be an optimal currency area (OCA). Evidence of the problems faced following the global financial crisis, with some eurozone members struggling because they were unable to adopt the macroeconomic policies they needed since they were tied to pursuing the same monetary policy as other members, suggest that the eurozone is not an OCA.

Evaluating globalisation and the WTO

Globalisation facilitates increased trade and in doing so has the potential to increase world output and improve material standard of living as a result of enabling countries to exploit their comparative advantage and firms to benefit from economies of scale.

However, in some nations there is much fear surrounding globalisation, in particular its potential to lead to job losses as a result of competition faced from low-cost countries. The World Trade Organization (WTO) which is responsible for promoting global free trade, is subject to significant criticism from developed nations, which want to keep more protectionist measures in place.

The WTO has also come under criticism from many LDCs for its inability to make substantial progress in reforming the agriculture sector. Primary sector-dependent LDCs, despite having a comparative advantage in this field, often struggle to compete with heavily subsidised agricultural products from the world's most developed nations, with the EU's Common Agricultural Policy and vast sums of money spent on agricultural subsidies in the USA meaning smaller nations are subjected to unfair competition in this area. Overall, while there are clearly long-term economic gains to be enjoyed from free trade, the transition can in the short term create pain that makes the move towards it politically unattractive.

In recent years concerns regarding globalisation have spread beyond the economic impact it can have. In particular, the transportation of goods across the world is contributing to rising pollution and has the potential to cause long-term environmental damage. Moreover, the incentives LDCs have to reduce the minimum environmental standards firms have to comply with in order to attract the crucial MNC investment they need to develop provide strong evidence for the need for greater regulation to prevent further environmental harm.

Exam tip

A big criticism of the WTO is that it is controlled by the world's biggest economies, meaning trade deals reached are often skewed in their favour. The WTO has been criticised for failing to achieve the agricultural reform that LDCs need because it is not in the developed nations' best interests to do so.

Summary

After studying the topic of *The global context* you should be able to:

- Explain the causes of globalisation.
- Evaluate the impact of multinational firms and globalisation on the performance of developed, developing and emerging economies.
- Explain what determines the terms of trade, including the Heckscher–Ohlin theory.
- Evaluate comparative advantage as an explanation of global trade patterns.
- Evaluate, using diagrams, the effectiveness of different methods of protectionism, including tariffs and quotas.

- Explain, with examples, the stages of economic integration — free trade areas, customs unions, monetary union and economic union.
- Evaluate the internal and external consequences of economic integration, including a diagrammatic analysis of trade creation and trade diversion.
- Understand how the European Union has evolved and evaluate the advantages of membership of the European Union and the single currency.
- Evaluate the role of the WTO in promoting free trade.

The financial sector

The role of the financial sector in the real economy

Money in the modern economy

Functions of money

Money fulfils four important functions in the economy:

- **Medium of exchange** — without money all transactions would have to take place by a barter system, where goods and services are exchanged for each other. This would make transactions very difficult because the goods involved in the transaction would need to be of equal value and each of the goods would have to be desired by the other party in the transaction. Money therefore facilitates the exchange of goods and services as it is accepted in all transactions by all parties.
- **Store of value** — if money did not hold its value individuals would not be willing to exchange goods and services for it. While other assets (such as property and paintings) also act as a store of value, money is an attractive store of value because it is easily transportable and is accepted in all transactions.
- **Unit of account** — money provides a common measure of the value of goods and services being exchanged, enabling producers and consumers to make decisions when selling and purchasing.
- **Standard of deferred payment** — goods and services can be paid for over time through loans, where economic agents commit to making a future monetary payment.

Knowledge check 15

How would hyperinflation undermine the functions of money?

Characteristics of money

In order to fulfil its functions money must have certain characteristics:

- **Portability** — must be easy to carry.
- **Divisibility** — must be dividable into small parts in order to complete transactions.
- **Acceptability** — must be accepted by economic agents in order to act as a medium of exchange.
- **Scarcity** — cannot be in unlimited supply or easily counterfeited.
- **Durability** — needs to be able to withstand wear and tear.
- **Stability in value** — value of money must remain relatively stable over time to act as a store of value.

Over time a number of commodities have acted as money, including gold. While it fits the characteristics of being divisible, acceptable, scarce and durable, it is clearly not portable and is subject to volatile fluctuations in its price, meaning it does not hold a stable value.

Narrow and broad money

While it is relatively easy to measure the quantity of coins and notes in circulation, it is much more difficult to measure the other assets that also fulfil the functions of money, such as bank deposits and financial assets, each of which have different degrees of **liquidity**.

> **Liquidity** The extent to which an asset can be converted to make a payment in the short term without the holder incurring a loss.

There are two primary methods that can be used to measure the money supply:

- **Narrow money (M0)** — this includes all notes and coins in circulation. Narrow money is highly liquid as it can be used to pay for transactions directly. However, the rise in the volume of electronic payments in recent years has rendered narrow money an outdated method of measuring the money supply and therefore the Bank of England stopped recording it in 2005.
- **Broad money (M4)** — this is a measure of the money stock which includes M0 together with wholesale and retail deposits held with monetary financial institutions such as banks. This measure reflects the fact that there are lots of assets that are 'near-money', in that they can be easily converted into cash for transactions. Money held in current accounts is an example of this — it is a highly liquid asset as most sellers now will accept payment by debit card to purchase a good or service. Money held in a savings account is also relatively liquid as it can be withdrawn to purchase goods or services, although there may be some time delay or a penalty attached to doing this, particularly if held in a savings account that pays a high interest rate on the basis of the deposit not being withdrawn for a fixed period of time.

The credit creation multiplier

Individuals and institutions are incentivised to place deposits with banks because they earn interest on these deposits. Knowing that it is unlikely that all depositors will require their money back at any one time, commercial banks make profit by reissuing a proportion of their deposits as loans, on which they charge a higher interest rate than they are paying their depositors.

The behaviour of commercial banks can have an important impact on the money supply. Suppose the government increases the money supply and uses it to finance the building of a new hospital. The firm that builds the hospital will deposit some of this money with a bank. The bank will lend out a proportion of this to borrowers. Borrowers then undertake expenditure, which will work its way back to banks in the form of higher deposits made by the firms that sell the goods and services purchased by the borrowers. This then enables the bank to further increase the supply of credit. This process is known as the credit creation multiplier — a process by which an increase in the money supply can have a multiplied effect on the amount of credit in an economy.

All banks will have a desired liquidity ratio — the proportion of their assets they choose to hold in liquid (cash) form. Suppose this is 60%. In this instance the credit creation multiplier will be relatively small — when the bank receives an extra £1,000 in deposits, it uses only £400 of this for new loans. When it gets £400 extra in deposits in the next round it will give out only £160 in new loans — the majority is kept as cash. Therefore, the smaller the liquidity ratio, the larger the credit creation multiplier will be. It can be calculated as follows:

1 ÷ Liquidity ratio

This means it is relatively difficult for the central bank to control the money supply, particularly as it will not know the liquidity ratios of each commercial bank and the fact that targeted liquidity ratios will change over time.

Determining the interest rate

The demand for money

There are a number of factors that determine the demand for money:

- **Transactions demand for money** — money is needed to purchase goods and services. The higher an individual's income, the more transactions they will wish to undertake and the higher the demand for money will be.
- **Precautionary demand for money** — individuals and firms want to hold some liquid assets to fund any emergency payment or spending opportunity that may arise in the future.
- **Speculative demand for money** — if share or bond prices are thought to be unreasonably high (meaning interest rates are low), individuals may choose to speculate by selling shares or bonds in order to hold money, speculating that in the future they will be able to repurchase these shares or bonds at lower prices.
- **Opportunity cost of holding money** — when individuals or firms choose to hold money they are sacrificing the interest they could have earned if the money had been invested. The higher the interest rate, the greater the opportunity cost of holding money is and the lower the demand for money will be. This explains how some of the other determinants of demand may change — for example, when the interest rate falls, the precautionary demand for money may increase as individuals will be more willing to hold cash in reserve when the cost of doing so has fallen.

Liquidity preference theory

If given a choice between how to hold their wealth, individuals would *ceteris paribus* prefer to hold money as opposed to other assets because it is the most liquid asset. The fact that individuals can earn interest on other assets is what incentivises them to limit their money holdings, meaning demand for money is determined by the interest rate.

Knowledge check 16

Suppose a bank receives an extra £350 in deposits and immediately increases its lending by £250 as a result of this. Calculate the total increase in bank lending that would result from the government increasing the money supply by £5 million.

The demand for money will decrease as the interest rate rises. This is because as the opportunity cost of holding money (the interest which could have been earned from holding an alternative asset) increases, individuals will be more willing to reduce their money holdings in order to earn interest from a less liquid asset. This means the demand curve for money is downward sloping and, assuming the supply of money is fixed at M^*, gives a money market equilibrium interest rate of r^*, as shown in Figure 19.

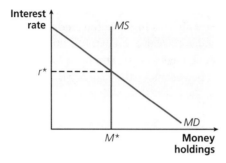

Figure 19 The money market

Loanable funds theory

While for individuals the interest rate represents the opportunity cost of holding money, for firms it more typically represents the cost of borrowing. The most significant borrowing undertaken by firms is to finance investment projects. The higher the interest rate, the worse the return from the investment and, therefore, the lower the demand for loanable funds will be. This means the investment schedule is downward sloping.

Households are the suppliers of loanable funds. The higher the rate of interest, the greater the supply of loanable funds will be. This is because at higher interest rates households will be more incentivised to save because the opportunity cost of holding or spending money will be high. This means the savings schedule is upward sloping.

The market for loanable funds therefore equilibrates at an interest rate of r^*, as shown in Figure 20.

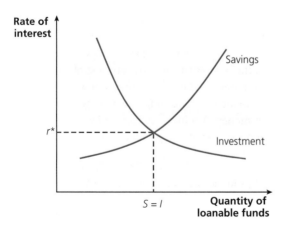

Figure 20 The market for loanable funds

The quantity theory of money

The concept of the velocity of money — the speed with which the money stock changes hands — is crucial in understanding the impact changes in the money supply have on the real economy.

The velocity of money is equal to:

$$V = PY \div M$$

where:

- V = velocity of money
- P = price level
- Y = real output
- M = money stock

Because $P \times Y$ is equal to nominal GDP, which effectively represents the volume of transactions in the economy, it is logical that the velocity of money must equal the volume of transactions divided by the money stock — the smaller the stock of money, the more often money must be changing hands in order to complete a given volume of transactions.

Multiplying both sides of this equation by M gives you the Fisher equation of exchange, named after economist Irving Fisher:

$$MV = PY$$

Classical economics assumes that the velocity of money (V) will be constant over time, as will real output (Y), which always tends towards the natural rate. This therefore provides a direct link between the money supply (M) and the price level (P), suggesting that increases in the money supply only serve to increase the rate of inflation in the economy.

It is important to recognise that the quantity theory of money works in explaining the macroeconomy only if the velocity of money is indeed constant and if real output does always revert to the natural rate. Given that Keynesians argue that the demand, and therefore the velocity, of money is volatile and that the economy does not always return to equilibrium, it is clear that there are some circumstances under which this direct relationship between money and the price level is questioned.

Nominal and real interest rates

In addition to the equation of exchange, Fisher proposed a relationship between the rate of inflation and the rate of interest:

$$i = r + \pi$$

where:

- i = nominal interest rate
- r = real interest rate
- π = inflation rate

This is best explained by a simple numerical example. Suppose the nominal interest rate paid on savings was 4% and the inflation rate was zero. It would be fair to conclude that an individual saving £1,000 in a bank was indeed earning 4% interest

---

Knowledge check 17

Using an aggregate demand and aggregate supply diagram, explain the likely impact of an increase in the money supply using the classical interpretation of the quantity theory of money.

from this investment as, in a year's time, a good that cost £1,000 a year earlier would still cost £1,000 but the individual would now have £1,040 as a result of saving for a year.

Let us now consider what would happen if the rate of inflation increased to 1% and the nominal interest rate increased to 5%. While the individual saving £1,000 would now have £1,050 at the end of the year, given that a good that cost £1,000 a year earlier would now cost £1,000, the individual is in real terms earning only 4% interest.

Therefore, in order for the real interest rate to be positive, the nominal interest rate must exceed the rate of inflation.

Financial institutions

The financial sector performs a crucial role in the modern economy. Firms need to borrow to finance investment and households need to borrow to finance expenditure. This finance is provided by financial intermediaries — financial institutions, which provide the link between borrowers and lenders. Banks are the most prominent financial institutions and can be categorised into three types:

- **Retail banks** — provide branch and internet banking services to households and small firms.
- **Wholesale banks** — operate on a larger scale than retail banks, taking deposits and making loans to large companies and other banks.
- **Universal banks** — financial deregulation resulted in many retail banks seeking to expand their operations to increase profits, meaning many banks today can best be described as universal banks, carrying out traditional retail bank functions alongside more complex and larger-scale investment banking operations.

Banks make a profit by incentivising individuals and firms to place deposits with them by paying a rate of interest on deposits. A proportion of these deposits is then loaned out at a higher interest rate, enabling banks to make a return. Clearly, the greater the proportion of deposits loaned out, the greater the profits will be, but such behaviour comes with increased risk. Banks must ensure they have a sufficient **liquidity ratio** to meet the demands of depositors wishing to withdraw funds at any particular time.

In the short term banks can borrow from each other to maintain their liquidity ratio. This is known as interbank lending and such loans made on the London interbank market are charged at the London Interbank Offered Rate (LIBOR) interest rate. An alternative is for banks to sell financial assets to the central bank or other banks and repurchase them at an agreed future date. These sale and repurchase agreements are known as repos, and act like a loan.

In recent times a new type of financial intermediary — pay-day lenders — has appeared on the landscape. These firms, such as Wonga (a large pay-day lender whose name inspired the term 'Wonga banking'), charge high interest rates sometimes equivalent to more than 1,000% per annum and make short-term loans to individuals who for whatever reason cannot access traditional forms of credit. There exists significant debate over whether such lenders are fulfilling an important function traditional banks cannot provide or whether they exist to profit from individuals suffering from financial hardship.

> **Exam tip**
>
> In the years immediately following the 2008 global financial crisis when the Bank of England cut the rate of interest to 0.5% and inflation peaked at more than 4%, real interest rates were positive. Make sure you can explain the implications of this in an exam — such a situation created very little incentive to save, as individuals were in real terms losing money from delaying expenditure!

> **Liquidity ratio** The ratio of liquid assets to total assets.

Forms of borrowing

There are a number of ways in which individuals can access finance, with the interest rate charged varying depending upon the type of borrowing being undertaken:

- **Mortgages** — long-term loans taken out for house purchases. Because the loan is secured against the value of the property, this is the type of borrowing on which the lowest interest rate tends to be charged, because it represents little risk to the lender.
- **Personal loans** — unsecured personal loans, typically ranging in value from £1,000 to £25,000, have a higher interest rate attached to them because there is no collateral in place to cover default. Personal loans tend to be given for a specific time period with fixed monthly repayments.
- **Overdrafts** — an arrangement which allows a bank's customer to spend more than is covered by current deposits at a pre-announced rate of interest up to an agreed limit.
- **Credit cards** — these can be used for payment of everyday transactions, with borrowers able to keep the finance indefinitely providing they meet minimum monthly repayments, usually covering the interest charged on the borrowing.

Knowledge check 18

The rate of interest charged on overdrafts is significantly higher than that charged on mortgages and personal loans. Why might this be?

The financial sector in developing and emerging economies

Harrod–Domar model

Most developing economies strive to achieve significant and sustained economic growth in order to tackle poverty and improve the population's standard of living. However, a limited productive capacity often acts as a constraint, which is why increasing long-run aggregate supply in order to expand the economy's productive potential is such an important focus for developing nations. High levels of investment are needed to achieve this.

The Harrod–Domar model proposes that a stable growth path is dependent on the savings ratio and the productivity of capital. This is because savings provide the crucial funds needed for investment. While some investment is required simply to replace depreciating capital and maintain the existing productive capacity, any investment above this level enables capital to accumulate and technology to be improved. This will lead to a subsequent increase in output and incomes. As income rises this generates increases in saving, causing the cycle to repeat itself. Increasing the savings ratio is therefore critical in achieving economic growth.

Evaluating Harrod–Domar

There are a number of important limitations that must be addressed when evaluating the importance of the Harrod–Domar model of economic development:

- **Transforming savings into investment** — in order to be able to do this, borrowers need to be able to get access to funds. The undeveloped nature of financial markets in LDCs means that saving often takes place outside of financial institutions, meaning it cannot be transformed into productive investment. This lack of a developed banking system is worsened in some nations by the government keeping interest rates low in an attempt to encourage firms to borrow, which

Exam tip

While the Harrod–Domar path to development may seem straightforward, it is not straightforward for most LDCs to adopt. When incomes are low, most resources are inevitably devoted to consumption, meaning the savings ratio remains low and the increase in the capital stock cannot commence.

disincentivises those that do have access to financial markets from participating in saving. Moreover, even if funds for borrowing are available, entrepreneurs are required to take risks with these funds in order to undertake investment. LDCs lacking entrepreneurship may require this to come in the form of immigrants or MNCs to enable economic development to occur.

- **Foreign exchange gap** — once firms have the funds for investment, they will need access to capital. Because LDCs have a limited capacity to produce capital goods, they will rely on importing them from developed nations. However, given that many LDCs find it difficult to earn sufficient foreign exchange to purchase these crucial imports required to enable manufacturing activity to expand, this creates a foreign exchange gap, which hinders development. The East Asian economies that were able to enjoy rapid development focused heavily on promoting international trade to increase exports and generate the foreign exchange needed to import capital goods.

- **Human capital** — there is a need for skilled labour to operate the capital goods. Relatively disappointing growth rates even for those countries that have access to capital highlight the problems caused by a weak education infrastructure. Indeed, a feature of the Asian tiger economies, which enjoyed rapid economic growth, such as Singapore and South Korea, was a high-quality education system.

Ultimately, the main barrier to developing nations pursuing the Harrod–Domar path to development is a lack of domestic savings. This means LDCs rely on external finance, in the form of overseas assistance, multinational investment or international borrowing, in order to be able to provide the funds needed to enact the development process.

Knowledge check 19

Identify the potential problems of relying on overseas assistance, multinational investment or international borrowing to provide the funds needed for investment.

Microfinance

Information failure resulting from urban commercial banks lacking the information they need to assess loan applications and the insecurity of property rights resulting in individuals not having sufficient collateral to borrow against means that many LDCs suffer from a lack of access to the formal financial sector in rural areas. This makes it difficult to raise funds for investment to improve agricultural productivity, as individuals have to enter informal credit markets where they are often charged high interest rates by monopoly local moneylenders who know villagers cannot access finance elsewhere.

In 1976 economist Muhammad Yunus launched the Grameen Bank, pioneering a microfinance solution to this problem, which involved making small-scale loans to groups of at least five women who were made jointly responsible for paying back the loans. This funding was primarily channelled to women because they were considered to invest more carefully and repay more reliably. The scheme resulted in great success, with high repayment records and significant small-scale investment resulting.

Similar schemes involved groups of households coming together to pool their savings in order to accumulate enough funds to launch small projects. Members of these groups take it in turns to use their joint savings, repaying the loan in order for the next person in the group to gain access to finance — this is known as a rotating savings and credit scheme (ROSCAS). Schemes of this nature do of course rely on trust between members, who have to be confident that once a member has benefited they will continue to make payments into the group savings to allow future members to benefit.

International financial flows

Many countries rely on international borrowing to generate the funds needed for investment. However, such borrowing inevitably results in an accumulation of debt that has caused a problem for a number of developing countries, particularly those in sub-Saharan Africa. In the late 1970s, when many LDCs sought external finance to overcome balance of payments problems, they chose to take loans from commercial sources charged at variable interest rates to avoid some of the conditions attached to IMF loans. When interest rates increased in the late 1980s as a result of a tightening of monetary policy around the world, this created a debt crisis in some LDCs, particularly in Latin America, where some nations threatened to default on their debt.

The cause of this crisis can be attributed to a poor use of borrowed funds. In order for international borrowing to be sustainable the funds it generates must be challenged into productive investment, which results in economic growth and increased export earnings. However, because of the unstable political environment in many LDCs there is often no incentive for governments to invest in long-term infrastructure projects, instead spending money on projects which advance short-run political objectives. Corruption in some countries meant that some funds were even diverted for personal use by government officials, providing no benefit to the economy whatsoever.

The result was that many developing nations faced debt crises, with a significant share of export revenue being used to pay the interest owed on historical debts. Initially, the World Bank favoured a debt restructuring programme, where countries were given longer to pay back, over a debt forgiveness programme.

The problem continued to worsen, to such an extent that at the 2005 G8 summit the world's richest economies agreed to cancel the debt owed by the world's most heavily indebted countries as part of the Heavily Indebted Poor Countries (HIPC) initiative.

Evaluating the role of the financial sector in economic development

The Harrod–Domar model demonstrates the importance of savings and investment in generating economic growth. If these funds cannot be raised domestically or in the form of FDI or overseas assistance, the financial sector has the ability to play a crucial role in fuelling economic development. Borrowing enables developing countries to invest in crucial physical and social infrastructure, such as transportation networks, education and healthcare. Countries such as Korea and Singapore are examples of nations that have used the financial sector by encouraging saving to achieve economic development, channelling the funds effectively to productive investment and infrastructure spending. Similarly, China enjoyed years of rapid economic growth, having been successful in attracting significant inflows of foreign direct investment.

One could argue that the continued slow economic development of sub-Saharan African economies, which also have poorly developed financial sectors, demonstrates the importance of the financial sector in economic development. However, there are a couple of important caveats to this argument. The first is that many sub-Saharan nations were in fact able to raise significant finance from abroad, but were simply unable to use it to generate development because they were badly channelled.

Exam tip

Historically the World Bank was reluctant to agree to debt forgiveness because it presents a moral hazard — if a country expects its debt to be forgiven, it will have no incentive to behave responsibly.

Moreover, while the East Asian economies made great use of the financial sector, they also started from a position of having a reasonably well-developed healthcare and education system.

Therefore, while a functional financial sector is a necessary condition in achieving economic development, it is clearly not a sufficient condition — a number of other conditions are also required.

The role of the central bank

Functions of a central bank

While the role and responsibilities vary between countries, a central bank often carries out a number of core functions, including acting as a banker to the government and commercial banks, issuing currency and fulfilling a role in regulating the financial system.

The Bank of England is the UK's central bank. Its main purpose is to promote the monetary and financial stability of the economy; this means it is required to keep prices stable and ensure there is an effective flow of funds in the economy for there to be confidence in financial institutions. To maintain this confidence the Bank of England acts as a banker to the commercial banks, operating an interbank lending market designed to equalise any imbalances in transactions between major banks on a daily basis. The Bank is also required to act as a lender of last resort, where it is prepared to lend to banks if they cannot obtain funds elsewhere, albeit at a penalty rate, in order to ensure banks have sufficient liquidity to carry out their activities.

In addition, the Bank of England has the following responsibilities:

- **Issues notes and coins** — controls the issue of banknotes to ensure demands for money are met without causing inflation.
- **Banker to the government** — the Bank handles all items of tax revenue and government expenditure on behalf of the government.
- **Managing the exchange rate** — while the Bank manages the UK's foreign currency reserves on behalf of the Treasury, it is important to note such reserves are rarely used to manage the exchange rate; the pound sterling is left to find its own level in the foreign exchange market.

Central bank independence

One of the first acts carried out by the Labour government upon election in 1997 was to grant the Bank of England independence. The Bank was given autonomy to set interest rates in order to achieve an inflation target set by the government (currently a symmetrical target of 2% as measured by the Consumer Price Index). Central bank independence, it was argued, would improve expectations about the future course of the macroeconomy, as it would limit the ability of the government to manipulate the economy to create political business cycles and would instead declare a pre-commitment to controlling inflation. The Monetary Policy Committee (MPC) meets monthly to set the interest rate.

While central bank independence should have improved the credibility of monetary policy, there are concerns that the central bank may pursue policy that causes harm

Exam tip

In some countries the central bank operates independently of the government, subject to achieving specific targets set by the government. This is the case in the UK, where the Bank of England has a range of delegated powers designed to achieve an inflation target set by the government.

to the government's other macroeconomic objectives, given that it is tasked primarily with price stability. This potential problem has to an extent been overcome by the Bank of England being instructed to achieve its inflation target subject to supporting the wider economic policy of the government, including objectives for growth and employment.

Policy measures

In the pre-crisis period (1997–2007), the Bank of England used the interest rate as its policy tool to achieve a rate of inflation within a 1% range either side of the inflation target, which was set at 2.5% measured by the Retail Price Index (RPI) from 1997–2003 and 2% measured by the Consumer Price Index (CPI) from 2004 onwards.

The Bank used open market operations to ensure short-run interest rates were kept in line with the Bank rate of interest. For example, in situations where liquidity shortages in the financial system were driving up market interest rates, the Bank intervened by purchasing securities (Treasury bills or gilts) in the open market, which released liquidity and pushed down market interest rates.

Except for two months when the inflation rate was marginally outside of the specified 1% range either side of the target, monetary policy was largely successful during this period, with the main objective of price stability clearly achieved.

However, since the 2008 financial crisis the policy environment has been significantly more challenging. In 2008 the rate of inflation accelerated, driven by an increase in food and commodities worldwide. Rather than raising interest rates in response to this, the MPC decided to cut rates, judging the causes of inflation to represent a temporary rather than a permanent shock and anticipating a slowdown in economic growth.

The financial crisis also fundamentally changed the operation of money markets. For many years in the USA mortgage lending had been based on the assumption of constantly rising house prices; when these started to fall, defaults increased, putting pressure on lenders. Speculation about the increased fragility led to investors withdrawing funds from banks, causing financial institutions to have liquidity problems. However, the size of these institutions and their ability to have far-reaching impacts on the economy effectively rendered them too big to fail, forcing the Bank of England to intervene to provide emergency finance to keep banks afloat — this is often referred to as the bank bail-out.

Liquidity constraints created problems in the interbank lending market, pushing up the interest rates in this market. With the Bank rate already at a record low of 0.5%, the Bank of England was unable to effectively fulfil its role as the lender of last resort. To plug this liquidity gap it therefore introduced a new policy of quantitative easing, whereby it issued Treasury bills to create central bank reserves and used these to purchase high-quality financial assets with the aim of providing additional liquidity to financial markets. This is essentially a method of increasing the money supply. By the end of 2014 the Asset Purchase Facility (APF), a subsidiary company of the Bank of England, had purchased £375 billion of assets by the creation of central bank reserves.

Knowledge check 20

What is the difference between the RPI and CPI measures of inflation?

Exam tip

During the crisis years the Bank of England faced a serious policy dilemma. On the one hand it wanted to control inflation, which would require an increase in interest rates, while on the other it needed to stimulate bank lending and promote an economic recovery. Ultimately, the latter objective was prioritised, explaining why interest rates stayed at record lows throughout a period of high inflation.

Financial regulation

Inadequate regulation of financial institutions is often cited as a key cause of the financial crisis. In the pre-crisis period, securitisation — a process by which banks bundle together stocks of assets such as residential mortgages into a bond — was used by banks to enable them to increase lending by reducing their liquidity ratios. The problem is that many of the assets that were securitised were risky (for example, sub-prime lending), meaning the bonds did not mature to be worth the amount expected. When this occurred it caused banks to tighten their lending, causing a liquidity crisis in the interbank lending market which left banks unable to meet the demands of depositors.

Crucially, financial institutions found themselves with an insufficient capital-adequacy ratio — the ratio of the bank's capital to the value of its risk-weighted assets. This is largely attributed to financial deregulation, which allowed banks to build up portfolios of risky lending which they did not have sufficient capital to cover, therefore contributing to the financial crisis.

In order to prevent such problems happening in the future, a new regulatory framework was introduced in April 2013, with a number of new bodies created:

- **Prudential Regulation Authority (PRA)** — responsible for **microprudential regulation**, working at the level of the individual firm to promote the safeness and soundness of deposit takers, insurers and major investment firms.
- **Financial Conduct Authority (FCA)** — responsible for ensuring markets function correctly, overseeing the conduct of firms not supervised by the PRA, such as asset managers, hedge funds and independent financial advisers.
- **Financial Policy Committee (FPC)** — responsible for **macroprudential regulation**, working to remove or reduce systemic risks in order to improve the resilience of the UK's financial system. It also has a secondary responsibility to support the government's economic policy, so must balance stabilising the financial system with facilitating economic growth and low unemployment. It has a range of powers at its disposal to achieve this, such as using a countercyclical capital buffer, which requires banks, building societies and large investment firms to hold additional loss-absorbing capital in times of need.

International financial regulation

Globalisation means large financial services firms now operate across the world. While the ease of transactions resulting from technological advancement has improved the efficiency with which markets can operate, it has of course increased the risk of contagion — the potential for a financial crisis in one country to spread and causing crises in other countries. The interconnected nature of financial markets across the world therefore justifies the need for international coordination of financial regulation, There are a number of organisations in place to do this:

- **Bank for International Settlements (BIS)** — established in 1930, initially to settle debate surrounding the controversial reparation payments imposed on Germany at the end of the First World War, its focus has changed over time and it now acts as a banker to the central banks, playing a key role in brokering financial agreements and promoting monetary cooperation between countries. The potential for financial contagion illustrated by the global financial crisis has resulted in more

Microprudential regulation Financial regulation intended to set standards and supervise financial institutions at the level of the individual firm.

Macroprudential regulation Financial regulation intended to mitigate the risks in the financial system as a whole.

coordinated action, with the latest Basel III agreement specifying internationally agreed capital adequacy requirements for banks. These rules are administered by individual central banks.

- **International Monetary Fund (IMF)** — established in 1945 at the Bretton Woods conference at the end of the Second World War, it initially had a specific brief to provide short-term assistance to countries experiencing balance of payments problems. Countries are able to seek loans from the IMF to finance a deficit on the balance of payments, in doing so agreeing to conditions imposed by the IMF designed to deal with the deficit, such as restrictive fiscal and monetary policies. Such loans were particularly important to countries during the period of fixed exchange rates, as they provided an alternative to having to devalue the currency. In recent years the government has provided loans to countries to prevent sovereign default, such as the finance provided to Greece in 2010. Loans have also been provided to governments that need funds to bail out private banks.

- **World Bank** — also established in 1945 at the Bretton Woods conference, it exists to provide longer-term funding for projects that will promote economic development. Such finance is provided at commercial interest rates on projects commercial banks would perceive as being too risky. These loans are particularly important to LDCs, which struggle to attract external finance, although they are sometimes criticised for building up unmanageable debt burdens within these nations.

Summary

After studying the topic of *The financial sector* you should be able to:
- Explain the functions and characteristics of money.
- Use the liquidity preference theory and loanable funds theory to explain how the interest rate is determined.
- Explain the relationship between the money supply and the price level using the Fisher equation and evaluate the relevance of the quantity theory of money.
- Understand the role of different organisations operating in the financial sector and explain why interest rates differ depending upon the form of borrowing.
- Evaluate the role of the financial sector in the real economy.
- Explain the role of the financial sector in developing and emerging economies in promoting economic development.
- Evaluate the role of saving in promoting economic development using the Harrod–Domar model and explain how savings rates can be increased through microfinance, international capital flows and aid.
- Evaluate the impact of remittances on developing economies.
- Explain the role of a central bank and evaluate the impact of central bank independence.
- Explain and evaluate the effectiveness of the different policy measures available to a central bank to help it achieve its objectives.
- Evaluate the advantages and disadvantages of a central bank acting as the lender of last resort.
- Explain why financial institutions are regulated and how changes in the regulation of financial institutions may contribute towards financial crises.
- Evaluate the role of the IMF and the World Bank in regulating the global financial system.

Questions & Answers

This section provides an explanation of the structure of the A-level Component 2: Macroeconomics and Component 3: Themes in Economics exams, together with strategies for approaching the different types of questions you will encounter. This is followed by a series of sample questions covering all the question types — multiple-choice, data-response and essays. After all of these questions there are some example answers from students. You should practise all of these questions yourself and compare your answers to these while reading the detailed comments on the answers to improve your understanding of what is required to achieve full marks.

Assessment objectives

To succeed in this course you will need to be able to demonstrate your ability in the following assessment objectives:

AO	Key skill	Explanation	Weighting at A-level
1	Knowledge	Demonstrate knowledge of terms/concepts and theories/models.	22.5%
2	Application	Apply knowledge and understanding to various economic contexts.	25%
3	Analysis	Analyse issues within economics, showing an understanding of their impact on economic agents.	25%
4	Evaluation	Evaluate economic arguments and use qualitative and quantitative evidence to support informed judgements relating to economic issues.	27.5%

■ Component 2: Macroeconomics

This is examined by a 120-minute paper. There are 80 marks awarded for the paper; you therefore have approximately 90 seconds to answer each question.

The content covered in the paper will include everything in this book alongside the Year 1 Macroeconomics content covered in *Student Guide 2*.

The paper is split into three sections:

- **Section A — Data-response**

  You will be given a variety of stimulus material, which is most likely to focus on the macroeconomic performance of a particular country or group of countries. You will then be asked a series of questions related to this stimulus material which tests the full range of assessment objectives. Questions will range in value from straightforward 2-mark questions to an 8- and a 12-mark question, both of which are level marked in the same way as the essays.

The section is worth a total of 30 marks and you should aim to spend approximately 40 minutes on it.

- **Section B — Quantitative essay questions**

  You will be given a choice of two essay questions and must answer one of these. The answer will require you to demonstrate some quantitative skills, most likely through drawing a diagram.

  The essay is worth 25 marks and you should aim to spend approximately 40 minutes on it.

- **Section C — Qualitative essay questions**

  You will be given a choice of two essay questions and must answer one of these. These essays will not require you to demonstrate any quantitative skills but you may well find a diagram will support your discussion; relevant diagrams will be credited.

  The essay is worth 25 marks and you should aim to spend approximately 40 minutes on it.

Component 3: Themes in Economics

This is examined by a 120-minute paper. There are 80 marks awarded for the paper; you therefore have approximately 90 seconds to answer each question.

The content covered in the paper will include everything in the A-level Economics specification, summarised by all four *Student Guides*.

The paper is split into two sections:

- **Section A — Multiple-choice**

  You will be asked 30 multiple-choice questions covering the whole A-level Economics specification. These could require you to conduct simple calculations, interpret points on diagrams or recall knowledge about technical theory.

  Each question is worth 1 mark and you will have to select the correct answer from a choice of four options.

  You should aim to spend approximately 45 minutes on this section.

- **Section B — Data-response**

  You will be given a variety of stimulus material focusing on a particular theme. You will then be asked a series of questions related to this theme which tests the full range of assessment objectives and requires use of both micro and macroeconomic theory. Questions will range in value from straightforward 2-mark questions to level-marked 15-mark questions.

  The section is worth a total of 50 marks and you should aim to spend approximately 75 minutes on it.

Answering multiple-choice questions

When answering multiple-choice questions you should:

- Work through them quickly — remember you have only 90 seconds on average to complete each one. Some will take longer than this but that should be compensated by others which are much quicker to complete. Do not spend too long on any one question.

- Cover up the options when reading the question and see whether you can work out the answer before looking at the four options — this is often quicker than reading the options and getting distracted by those that are incorrect but are close to being right.
- If unsure, eliminate those answers you know to be incorrect and choose between any options you have left — there is no penalty for answering incorrectly so you should never leave an answer blank.
- When practising multiple-choice questions in the build-up to the exam, try to justify why the incorrect options are incorrect. This is done in the example multiple-choice questions in this guide.

Answering data-response questions

When answering data-response questions you should:

- Read the stimulus material very carefully, remembering to refer to it in your answers when required.
- Work out which assessment objectives the question is testing — do not waste time evaluating when the question is only asking you to offer an explanation.
- Make sure you always fully apply your answer to the circumstances in the question; you will need to reference the stimulus material throughout and should avoid producing bland technical answers which ignore the specific information given about the country/countries in the case study.

Answering essay questions

The most important thing to remember when answering essay questions is to cover each of the four skills tested by the assessment objectives. These essays, along with any questions that require evaluation in the data-response section, are level marked. Which level your answer is placed in depends upon how well you have covered each of the four skills — these are graded as being either 'Limited', 'Reasonable', 'Good' or 'Strong'. Aim to get into the 'Strong' category on all skills, as detailed below.

	AO1 and AO2	AO3	AO4
Limited	Awareness of the meaning of the terms in the question.	Simple statement(s) of cause and effect.	An unsupported assertion.
Reasonable	As above and applied to the context of the question.	An explanation of causes and consequences, which omit some key links in the chain of argument.	Some attempt to come to a conclusion, which shows some recognition of influencing factors.
Good	Precision in the use of the terms in the question and applied in a focused way to the context of the question.	An explanation of causes and consequences, developing most of the links in the chain of argument.	A conclusion is drawn weighing up both sides, but without reaching a supported judgement.
Strong		An explanation of causes and consequences, fully developing the links in the chain of argument.	A conclusion is drawn weighing up both sides, and reaches a supported judgement.

Generally, the best way to approach these questions is to fully analyse one side of the argument, analyse the other side and then reach a judgement saying which side of the argument is stronger and why you have reached this conclusion. This is likely to include a consideration of the factors your judgement depends upon.

■A-level Macroeconomics Section A

Data-response

Turbulence in the UK economy: financial crisis and the European debate

The global financial crisis resulted in a significant period of turbulence for the UK economy, as illustrated by the fluctuating growth rates evidenced in Table 1.

Table 1 UK Economics growth rate, 2005–14

Year	Annual % change in GDP	Year	Annual % change in GDP
2005	2.8	2010	1.9
2006	3	2011	1.6
2007	2.6	2012	0.7
2008	−0.3	2013	1.7
2009	−4.3	2014	2.6

The global financial crisis contributed to the most significant recession the UK economy has experienced since the Great Depression in the early 1930s. Changes in the regulatory environment in the financial sector are considered to be a significant cause of this. While in the 1960s and 1970s strict capital and liquidity ratios were applied to banks, along with a number of other rules designed to limit risky behaviour, from the 1980s significant financial deregulation occurred. This resulted in banks overleveraging, engaging in increasingly risky lending, which ultimately left financial institutions with insufficient capital reserves to continue to function without being 'bailed out'. Economists have since looked back to the boom in the early 2000s as being excessively debt fuelled. By 2006, households were even taking advantage of the cheaper interest rates offered on mortgages (4.5% compared with 14.5% on credit card debt) to take out mortgages which exceeded the value of their homes, with the extra capital being used to fund a range of home improvements and other expensive purchases, such as cars or foreign holidays. Banks were willing to lend up to 120% of the value of the home

to an individual because they believed that house prices were on a consistently rising path.

While financial deregulation was certainly a contributory factor to the recession, the 2015 general election campaign saw a significant debate over the role played by the tax and spending policies of the government in the build-up to the financial crisis, with public sector net debt increasing significantly during a period in which it was being greatly reduced in most other industrialised nations.

Since 2010 there has been evidence of improvement for the prospects of an economy with a population of 65 million people, comprised of a working-age population of 41.9 million. In October 2015 James Sproule, Chief Economist at the Institute of Directors, said: 'Improving jobs figures, with 31.2 million people now in work, and strong wage growth shows that the business-led recovery is well on track. Despite uncertainties at home and abroad, employers have continued to create jobs, raise productivity and boost pay in a vote of confidence in the British economy.'

TUC General Secretary Frances O'Grady welcomed this improving picture, but noted: 'It is also clear that there is still spare capacity in the jobs market. With inflation at zero and more than 1 million people in part-time work who would like to be in full-time employment, there is no case for immediate interest rate increases.' Matthew Whittaker, Chief Economist at the Resolution Foundation, echoes these sentiments, noting: 'There is significant variation in the extent to which this jobs revival has been shared across the country, with approximately 9 million individuals still recorded as being economically inactive. Many parts of the UK remain a long way short of their pre-recession levels.'

➜

With the macroeconomic outlook improving, the next major challenge that has the potential to create significant uncertainty and turbulence in the UK is the proposed referendum over the country's continued membership of the European Union. There exists significant debate among economists as to the potential impacts a 'Brexit' could have on the economy. Analysis by the Centre for Economic Performance calculated that the UK could suffer income falls of between 6.3% and 9.5% of GDP should voters opt to leave the European Union — a similar loss to that resulting from the 2008–9 global financial crisis. This was based on the assumption that the UK was not able to negotiate favourable trade terms upon exit; under an optimistic scenario in which the UK continues to have a free trade agreement (FTA) with the EU, losses are estimated to be smaller, at 2.2% of GDP.

Economist Tim Congdon takes a different view, highlighting the 'damage that excessive and misguided regulation is doing to British business, particularly to small and medium-sized businesses'. He concludes that the UK is roughly 11.5% of GDP worse off because it is a member of the EU instead of being a fully independent sovereign nation.

(a) Using Table 1, identify the two stages of the economic cycle the UK economy could be said to be operating in between 2008 and 2014. (2 marks)

ⓔ Use the data on growth rates to identify the years in which a particular stage of the economic cycle could be said to be occurring. Clearly separate the two different stages and periods within your answer.

(b) In 2006, the interest rate charged on mortgage repayments was approximately 4.5%, compared with the 14.5% interest rate charged on credit card repayments. Explain why the rate of interest varies in different money markets. (2 marks)

ⓔ First identify at least one factor that determines the rate of interest that is charged by a lender. Then explain how this factor differs in the mortgage and credit card markets in order to analyse why interest rates vary.

(c) Use the information in the case study to calculate the UK's unemployment rate in 2015. (2 marks)

ⓔ Look carefully through the case study to find the data you need to be able to calculate the unemployment rate. You may need to carry out some preliminary calculations before you are able to calculate the unemployment rate directly.

(d) Explain, using a relevant diagram, whether the UK economy has a negative output gap in 2015. (4 marks)

Begin by explaining what is meant by a negative output gap and look for supporting evidence in the case study to identify whether the UK economy does indeed have a negative output gap. Use an AD/AS diagram to support your answer, illustrating the position of the UK economy in 2015 and deciding on whether this demonstrates a negative output gap.

(e) Evaluate the role deregulation of the financial sector played in the UK economy experiencing its deepest recession since the Great Depression. (8 marks)

ⓔ Start by identifying what is meant by deregulation and explain the ways in which this process contributed towards the global financial crisis and the subsequent recession that resulted. The directive word 'evaluate' means you will need to question the significance of these arguments, perhaps by considering other factors that contributed towards the recession. The answer should end with a clear judgement where you reach a position concerning the importance of deregulation in explaining the economic downturn. This judgement must be fully supported.

(f) **Using evidence from the stimulus material, evaluate the extent to which the UK economy would benefit from exiting the European Union.** (12 marks)

ⓔ A two-sided answer is required here that considers both the costs and the benefits to the UK economy of leaving the European Union. Evaluation of these costs and benefits is required — think about how such arguments might be flawed and what conditions are required for them to hold. Your answer should then end with a clearly supported judgement justifying whether or not you believe the UK economy would benefit from exiting the European Union.

Student A

(a) Between 2008 and 2009 the UK economy was in the recession phase of the economic cycle. From 2010 to 2014 the UK economy was in the recovery phase of the economic cycle.

ⓔ **2/2 marks awarded.** The student correctly recognises that the contraction in GDP between 2008 and 2009 indicates the economy is in recession, with the growth that follows this in 2010 representing the start of the recovery phase.

(b) Lenders vary the interest rate according to the level of risk and security attached to the borrowing. Mortgages are secured loans — if an individual doesn't pay back their mortgage, lenders can repossess the house in order to recover the debt. When a loan is secured it reduces the risk to the bank of the money not being returned to it, which is why it is prepared to lend at lower interest rates than more risky lending on unsecured forms of debt such as credit cards.

ⓔ **2/2 marks awarded.** The two key concepts that determine interest rates — risk and security — are identified. There is then a strong explanation of why mortgages represent high-security and therefore low-risk lending, thus justifying why interest rates are lowest in this market. More could have been offered to explain the high interest rates charged on credit cards — the student could have considered what happens when an individual fails to repay a credit card debt.

(c) Unemployment rate = (number of unemployed ÷ labour force) × 100

Labour force = Working age population – Economically inactive = 41.9m – 9m = 32.9m

Unemployed = Labour force – Number of employed = 32.9m – 31.2m = 1.7m

Unemployment rate = (1.7m ÷ 32.9m) × 100 = 5.2%

ⓔ **2/2 marks awarded.** The student correctly calculates the size of the labour force by discounting the economically inactive from the working-age population. This answer is then used to calculate the number of individuals who are unemployed (any individuals who are of working age and in the labour force but are without work are classed as being unemployed). The correct formula for the unemployment rate is then used to arrive at the correct answer.

(d) A negative output gap occurs when an economy's actual output is below its potential output. The UK economy had a negative output gap in 2015 because the case study refers to there being significant spare capacity in the economy, referring to the 1 million people who are in part-time jobs but would like to be in full-time employment. The fact that there is 'spare capacity' is evidence of a negative output gap, as it indicates there are 'spare' factors of production that are not being fully utilised, suggesting the economy is not operating at maximum output. This is illustrated on the diagram below.

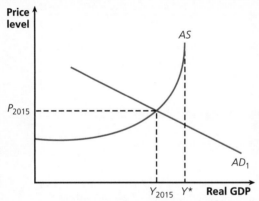

ⓔ **3/4 marks awarded.** A correct definition of a negative output gap is provided, with excellent use of the case study to provide supporting evidence that the UK economy is experiencing a negative output gap in 2015. The diagram is well labelled and clearly illustrates a negative output gap. However, the student does not explain the diagram within their answer. Reference to the diagram should be made to demonstrate the size of the negative output gap. Potential output is at $Y*$ with actual output only at Y_{2015}, meaning the negative output gap is equal to $Y* - Y_{2015}$.

(e) Financial deregulation is the removal of government rules controlling how banks and other financial institutions operate. Such deregulation began in the 1980s as part of wider moves to improve the productivity of the UK economy by allowing markets to function with less government intervention.

Faced with reduced regulation to limit their activities, financial institutions sought to increase their profits by reducing their liquidity ratios and engaging in a process known as securitisation — the bundling together of stocks of assets such as residential mortgages into a bond designed to provide a flow of income to the bond holder. However, in aggressively increasing the level of lending undertaken, this required banks to take risks and engage in 'sub-prime' lending, providing large loans to individuals who previously would not have had access to such finance. Inevitably individuals started to default on their repayments. When this happened banks found themselves with insufficient capital-adequacy ratios to absorb these losses, forcing the government to bail many of them out.

This was a major cause of recession in the UK. Bank lending tightened significantly, which, coupled with a crisis of confidence among consumers and investors, resulted in significant falls in aggregate demand. Had financial deregulation not taken place, much of the sub-prime lending would not have taken place initially and, even if it had, the banks would have had greater reserves with which they could tackle the problems when they arose.

The extent to which financial deregulation is responsible for the recession experienced by the UK does however depend upon whether improved financial regulation in the UK would have actually prevented the global financial crisis from occurring. This is questionable as the inter-linked nature of world economies means that many of the problems stemmed from sub-prime lending in the USA — something any amount of financial regulation in the UK would not have been able to do anything about. While greater regulation may have prevented UK institutions from suffering the problems they did, the UK economy still would have been harmed as a result of contagion.

In conclusion, financial deregulation has to be considered to be the most significant cause of the recession experienced in the UK. While the Financial Conduct Authority (FCA) was in place to regulate individual institutions, the lack of any macro-prudential regulation meant systemic risk was able to develop in the UK's financial system, resulting in the collapse of the banking sector that had far-reaching consequences.

ⓔ **6/8 marks awarded.** The student clearly understands what is meant by financial deregulation and the policy context in which this was occurring. Strong analysis is then offered of how financial deregulation resulted in the financial crisis, with an excellent understanding of the process of securitisation and the impact of sub-prime lending demonstrated. The link between problems in the financial sector and the real economy is well made. Strong evaluation is offered when the student recognises the limited ability of domestic financial regulation to impact upon global financial markets, while the judgement offers a clearly supported justification of why financial deregulation was such a significant cause of the financial crisis, illustrating the problems with the regulatory system focusing too heavily on the behaviour of individual firms rather than the whole financial system. The answer could be improved by drawing on other material from the case study to consider other factors that contributed to the recession experienced in the UK, such as the government's macroeconomic policies in the build-up to the global financial crisis.

(f) Perhaps the single biggest argument presented against the UK leaving the EU is that it will mean leaving the single market which enables free trade between member states. Given that EU countries account for nearly half of all Britain's exports, this could cause significant damage to the UK's economy. If British firms now find themselves facing barriers to trade this will reduce the international competitiveness of British goods and services, which will inevitably lead to exports falling. Protectionism will essentially prevent UK firms from fully exploiting comparative advantage, with the economies of scale that come from having access to a market of more than 500 million consumers potentially lost. This could have a damaging effect on output in the UK economy. Moreover, foreign direct investment (FDI) could fall. The UK currently receives significant inflows of FDI which could be in jeopardy if it is no longer a member of the single market. A number of large multinationals are headquartered in the UK because of the access it gives them to the European single market; exit from the EU could lead to a number of these firms relocating, which could significantly harm employment levels in the UK economy.

However, the strength of this point clearly depends upon whether the UK government is able to negotiate free trade deals with the European Union upon exit. As one of the world's largest economies the UK is an important export market for many EU countries, meaning there is a good chance the EU would be willing to reach free trade agreements with the UK. If this happens then the UK would effectively still be operating as part of the customs union, meaning international competitiveness would not be harmed in the way initially analysed.

Those in favour of an EU exit instead argue that international trade provides the strongest case for Britain leaving the European Union. Outside of the EU, Britain would be free to negotiate its own trade deals with emerging markets, enabling it to expand trade in areas of rapidly rising incomes. This is however assuming that the UK was able to negotiate more favourable deals than it currently has as being part of the EU and crucially would require trade to these countries to grow enough to offset any loss in trade with EU countries as a result of the exit.

Ultimately the UK is likely to benefit from leaving the European Union because it can only have a positive impact on trade. While leaving the single market will require the negotiation of new trade deals and as a result create some short-term uncertainty, the reality is that the size of the UK's economy will enable it to form agreements which enable it to trade freely with EU nations even when it exits. Trade with the EU will therefore not be harmed, while there are clear benefits to be found from having the sovereignty to be able to negotiate with emerging markets to expand trade in these countries with rapidly rising incomes.

@ **11/12 marks awarded.** The answer begins with strong analysis of the potentially damaging implications to international trade of the UK leaving the EU, with a well-developed explanation clearly outlining the benefits that come from being a member of the single market and the harmful implications on growth and employment an exit could cause. This point is then well evaluated; the student understands these disadvantages will hold only if leaving the EU results in protectionist measures being adopted by EU members against the UK. Strong analysis is offered of why the UK may benefit from leaving the EU by considering the beneficial impact this could have on trade with emerging markets; such benefits are then put into context by considering these potential gains against the losses that will occur from reduced trade with EU members. The judgement is excellent, drawing together the arguments made in the answer to clearly justify why leaving the EU would benefit the UK economy. The answer would however benefit from more breadth — implications other than those on trade are worth considering.

Student B

(a) There was negative economic growth in 2008 and 2009, meaning the economy was in recession. This was followed by positive economic growth from 2010, although the rate of this fluctuated and real output did not return to pre-recession levels.

🅮 **1/2 marks awarded.** This is a descriptive answer outlining the growth that took place between 2008 and 2014 without clear links to the phases of the economic cycle. Credit is awarded for recognising there was a recession between 2008 and 2009, but the student fails to go beyond recognising there was positive growth between 2010 and 2014.

(b) Lenders charge higher interest rates on credit cards because they are a more risky form of lending, because they are given to people less likely to pay back the money than those who receive mortgages, who tend to be older and wealthier.

🅮 **1/2 marks awarded.** The student is credited for identifying risk as a determinant of interest rates and linking this to credit card lending, which is considered relatively high risk for a bank. However, the explanation of why credit card lending is more risky consists of an unsubstantiated assertion — consideration of the difference between secured and unsecured lending would have improved this answer.

(c) Unemployment rate = 9 million ÷ 65 million × 100 = 13.8%.

🅮 **0/2 marks awarded.** The student confuses unemployment with economic inactivity. An individual who is of working age but is unwilling to work, perhaps because they are a full-time student or homemaker, is not classed as being unemployed because they are not part of the labour force. The denominator is also incorrect because it implies that individuals outside of working age can also be unemployed, which is not the case — the denominator must therefore be the labour force. The number of people in the population was not needed for this question.

(d) The fact that 9 million individuals are economically inactive is evidence of a negative output gap, as these individuals could be producing output. Moreover, the fact that output has still not returned to the pre-recession levels means that output is not as high as it could be — the economy is not producing at Y^*, which it would have to be if a negative output gap were not occurring.

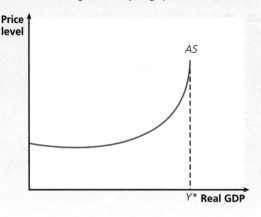

e 1/4 marks awarded. Economic inactivity is not in itself evidence of a negative output gap — those who are economically inactive are not in the labour force so do not represent spare factors of production. The answer lacks a clear technical definition of what a negative output gap is, but credit is given for correctly linking the concept to the idea that the economy is not yet at pre-recession levels of output, implying that actual output is below potential output. While the diagram illustrates the level of potential output in the economy, it cannot be credited as no indication is given of where actual output in the economy is.

(e) Financial deregulation meant there were insufficient checks and restrictions placed on the activity of financial institutions. This resulted in financial institutions engaging in reckless behaviour, providing huge loans (such as the example of 120% of the value of the house loans from the case study) to individuals who were unlikely to be able to afford to pay them back. When such individuals inevitably defaulted on their repayments, this created a number of problems in the financial system which led to a global financial crisis and the subsequent recession in the UK. Ultimately financial deregulation contributed to a debt-fuelled boom — when credit tightened, this left individuals and firms with insufficient finance to sustain the previously high levels of consumption and investment, in the process causing a prolonged recession.

However, in reality the financial crisis only resulted in problems in the real economy because of poor macroeconomic management during the years leading up to the financial crisis. During the boom years the government operated a small budget deficit, meaning national debt was increasing. When the financial crisis hit and automatic stabilisers came into effect, this inevitably increased the size of the deficit still further.

ⓔ 3/8 marks awarded. The student recognises deregulation represents the removal of rules but could be more specific on this. A reasonable analysis is then offered of how financial deregulation led to the explosion of credit and subsequent defaults and there is recognition that this resulted in credit tightening, which contributed to the recession. However, some links in this chain of analysis are missing — for example, there is no real explanation of how reckless lending resulted in a credit crunch. This really needs to be linked to the failure of banks to have sufficient capital adequacy ratios and the subsequent bank bail-outs this resulted in. There is limited evaluation as the student makes the valid point that the government was running a budget deficit before the financial crisis occurred, but there is no clear explanation of why this worsened the impact of the financial crisis. For good evaluation to be present the student would have to weigh up the relative significance of their arguments by reaching a judgement.

(f) The case study presents the argument by Tim Congdon that the UK economy could quite easily expand by more than 10% as a result of exiting the European Union. This is because of the significant benefits which come from not having to follow EU regulation. Currently as a member of the EU, the UK is obliged to enforce significant amounts of regulation on its firms. This can cause the costs of production of UK firms, particularly those of a small or medium size, to be higher than they would be outside of the EU, harming their ability to grow and compete internationally. By leaving the EU the UK would be free to set regulation as it sees fit, potentially freeing up firms to become more internationally competitive and in doing so increasing exports and improving the balance of payments.

Moreover, the UK economy would benefit from leaving the EU as it would no longer have to pay large contributions for membership. The UK is currently a net contributor to the EU; leaving could therefore reduce government spending and help to reduce national debt. An exit would also reduce the risk of contagion as it would enable the UK to create distance between itself and EU members, putting less pressure on it to contribute to any bail-outs of struggling EU nations.

Leaving the European Union would also give the UK control over its borders, preventing freedom of movement resulting in unwanted immigration. This however depends upon current levels of emigration by British citizens to other EU states; given that many British citizens currently choose to work and live in other EU countries, the impact on net immigration may not be as significant as first analysed.

ⓔ 6/12 marks awarded. There is a good analysis of the benefits that come from leaving the EU in terms of not having to follow EU regulation, although no details are given of the type of excessive regulation that is currently harming UK firms. Further arguments in favour of the UK leaving the EU are explored, but their strength is not considered — for example, while it is correct to say that the UK is a net contributor to the EU, the relatively small cost of this as a proportion of GDP is not considered. Reasonable evaluation is presented of why the immigration benefits that could result from an exit are relatively limited, although no consideration is given to the role of immigrants in filling skills shortages. The answer considers a number of points but does perhaps miss the most significant, in that there is no analysis of the trade implications of an exit. The answer also lacks a judgement.

A-level Macroeconomics Section B

Quantitative essay question

In October 2015 the UK government put into law a Fiscal Responsibility Charter, which commits the government to producing budget surpluses during periods of economic growth. It also required the government to be running a budget surplus by 2019–20. This act is seen as symbolic of the austerity economics implemented by the government, with a range of policy measures on the horizon designed to reduce government expenditure to eliminate the budget deficit. There exists much debate among economists over the relative merits of austerity economics.

Evaluate, using an appropriate diagram(s), the extent to which achieving a balanced budget is important in achieving the government's macroeconomic objectives. (25 marks)

ⓔ A two-sided discussion is required here that considers both the advantages and disadvantages of the government aiming to balance its budget. Traditionally, diagrammatic analysis using *AD/AS* should be included to illustrate the potential impacts of austerity economics on the government's macroeconomic objectives. The answer should go on to offer detailed evaluation, which considers the relative merits of the arguments made in analysis and explains the conditions under which the arguments may not hold. The answer should conclude with a supported judgement focused on the 'extent to which' element.

Student A

One of the main arguments in favour of pursuing austerity economics to achieve a balanced budget is the positive impact it can have on the levels of confidence within the economy. ⓐ Continuing to run a large budget deficit increases national debt, posing the risk of this debt becoming unsustainable. If concerns develop about the ability of the government to repay this debt, this can push up interest rates on borrowing to crippling levels, as was the case in Greece, which struggled to raise the external finance needed to keep its economy afloat. Austerity policies to control the deficit will therefore improve confidence in the economy, meaning the government can continue to borrow at low interest rates. ⓑ Aiming to balance the budget also improves the confidence of economic agents in the state of the economy. Consumers will see a declining budget deficit as evidence of an improved economic climate, encouraging them to spend more and thus raising consumption. Firms will also gain confidence from more credible government macroeconomic policy. ⓒ Anticipating economic growth in the future, they will therefore undertake more investment, causing investment to increase. As consumption and investment are both components of aggregate demand $(AD = C + I + G + X - M)$, this improved confidence in the economy will cause the aggregate demand curve to shift to the right, as illustrated in the diagram below. The result will be that output will increase from Y_1 to Y_2, causing economic growth and therefore achieving one of the government's macroeconomic objectives. Higher levels of output will increase the demand for labour, increasing employment and therefore achieving another of the government's objectives of reducing unemployment. ⓓ

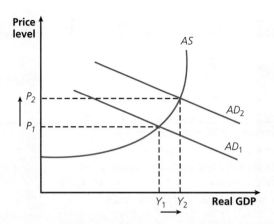

However, this depends upon whether the increases in aggregate demand generated from increased confidence offset any decreases in aggregate demand which may result from implementing the contractionary fiscal policies required in order to balance the budget. Realistically, a budget deficit can only be corrected by raising taxes on individuals, increasing taxes on firms, reducing government expenditure or a combination of all three policies. e Raising taxes on individuals will decrease consumption and raising corporation tax will reduce the profitability of investment and will therefore cause investment to fall. Given Consumption, Investment and Government Spending are all components of aggregate demand, austerity economics will therefore put pressures on aggregate demand to shift to the left — it is only if the impact on confidence is more significant that economic growth will actually be achieved as a result of these policies. f

Another benefit of aiming to balance the budget is that it will reduce debt interest repayments. When the government is spending less of its revenue servicing debt interest it will be able to increase its expenditure on infrastructure projects, potentially increasing the productive capacity of the economy and in doing so shifting out the aggregate supply curve. Combined with the shift in aggregate demand, this enables the economy to achieve substantial economic growth (from Y_1 to Y_2) and large increases in employment without causing inflationary pressures, as illustrated in the diagram below. g

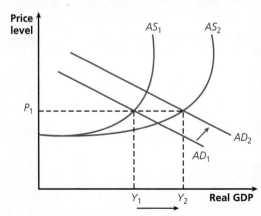

However, the extent to which pursuing a balanced budget results in the productive capacity of the economy increasing depends upon how long it takes for the balanced budget to be achieved. The question refers to the budget not being balanced until 2019–20. It is only once the budget has been balanced that debt interest payments will actually start to fall. Until then, infrastructure spending may in fact fall as the government attempts to reduce the level of public expenditure, meaning it may be many years until the positive impacts on aggregate supply are seen. Indeed, in the short run aggregate supply may fall as the government is forced to delay infrastructure projects in order to meet its target of balancing the budget. h

In judgement, pursuing austerity policies is unlikely to have a positive impact on the government's macroeconomic objectives. While reducing the level of national debt is important, the reality is that at a time when interest rates are at record lows, the government should not be overly concerned with high levels of borrowing but should instead be aiming to stimulate the economy. Moreover, it is questionable whether such policies will even result in the government achieving a balanced budget. As government expenditure falls it is likely that unemployment will rise, reducing the government's tax revenue and raising welfare expenditure. This could therefore render the policy highly ineffective. i

e **24/25 marks awarded.** a The student starts their answer by immediately identifying the key objective of austerity policies — to improve confidence in the economy. b A strong explanation is offered of the damage unsustainable national debt can do to an economy, with effective use of the Greece example. c The positive impact austerity policies have on consumer and business confidence is well explained. d Strong analysis is then presented by linking this improved confidence to the aggregate demand curve, with an accurate diagram well explained to demonstrate the impact targeting a balanced budget can have on economic growth and employment. e The student produces superb evaluation, recognising that these benefits will hold only if the confidence effect outweighs the decreases in the components of aggregate demand which are likely to result from austerity policies. f These potentially negative impacts are well detailed, leading the student to conclude that economic growth will not necessarily be achieved as a result of aiming to balance the budget.

g The answer goes on to consider the potentially positive impacts a balanced budget can have on aggregate supply, with an accurate diagram illustrating the impact this has on the economy's productive capacity. h This point is also well evaluated by considering the time frame under which the benefits are likely to be achieved. i The answer reaches a strong judgement, which questions both the premise of high levels of national debt being particularly problematic and the practicalities of aiming to achieve a balanced budget through pursuing austerity policies.

Student B

Balancing the budget is important in enabling the government to achieve intergenerational equality. Running a budget deficit will simply increase the national debt, increasing debt interest payments for future generations. Balancing the budget forces the current generation to live within their means and reduces the burden on future generations, therefore not harming standard of living in the future. This is important as it can be seen as pursuing a sustainable macroeconomic policy. a

However, the extent to which a budget deficit creates intergenerational inequality depends upon what government funds are being spent on. If the government is actually running a balanced budget on current expenditure and the deficit is simply comprised of capital expenditure then it could be argued that attempting to balance the budget could harm future generations, as it would result in reduced expenditure on long-term investment that will increase the productive capacity of the economy in the future. b

Moving from a position of a budget deficit to a balanced budget will inevitably result in aggregate demand falling — the government will be forced to raise taxes, causing consumption and possibly investment to fall. This will result in the aggregate demand curve shifting to the left, which will cause real output to fall, as shown in the diagram. c

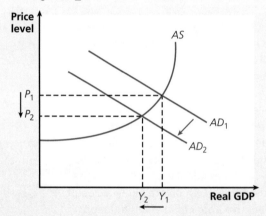

The impact of this depends upon the size of the multiplier effect. If the marginal propensity to save and the marginal propensity to import is high then the negative multiplier will be relatively small, meaning the decreases in aggregate demand and therefore economic growth will be less significant than if the multiplier were bigger. d

Ultimately, at a time when monetary policy cannot be used to stimulate the economy because interest rates are already near zero, it is even more important for expansionary fiscal policy to be used. e

e 11/25 marks awarded. **a** A good attempt is made to analyse the intergenerational impact of operating a balanced budget, with valid reference to the sustainability of macroeconomic policy. The student would however benefit from considering the direct and present impact austerity policies could have on the government's macroeconomic objectives of growth and low unemployment. **b** Reasonable evaluation is offered, recognising the difference between current and capital expenditure, although links to the government's main macroeconomic objectives remain absent. **c** Good analysis is offered on the potentially negative impact austerity policies could have on aggregate demand and therefore economic growth, but more detail could be given here. For example, the student could consider the harms of working against automatic stabilisers in this way and the need to be pursuing expansionary fiscal policies in times of sluggish growth. **d** A reasonable evaluation point is made concerning the size of the negative multiplier; this should be linked to the diagram to be fully developed. **e** The judgement has the potential to be excellent, as it offers some broader policy context justifying the need for expansionary fiscal policy. However, this is not related back to the question — the student needs to explain the implications of this conclusion for the merits of pursuing austerity policies to achieve a balanced budget.

■ A-level Macroeconomics Section C

Qualitative essay question

Introduced in April 2003, Child Tax Credits and Working Tax Credit are payments given to families raising children and to working individuals on low incomes. In 2015, more than 4 million individuals claimed these benefits, with the average tax credit award standing at £6,340 a year, representing approximately 14% of the welfare budget.

In late 2015 the government proposed a major overhaul of the tax credits system, designed to save approximately £4.5 billion. This would be done by reducing the income threshold at which individuals start to see their tax credits reduced and increasing the rate at which those payments are cut. These changes were proposed alongside raising the personal allowance on income tax, implementing a 'living wage' and improving the availability of childcare.

Evaluate the consequences of such policies on inequality and poverty. (25 marks)

ⓔ A two-sided discussion is required here which considers how these reforms could worsen or reduce inequality and poverty. You should aim to include reference to the Lorenz curve or the Gini coefficient within your answer, before going on to offer evaluation that recognises the limitations or conditions under which your analysis holds. The answer should end with a clearly supported judgement where you reach a definitive position on whether these policy measures are likely to reduce or worsen inequality and poverty.

Student A

Reducing tax credits will worsen inequality and poverty. Tax credits effectively act as a form of income redistribution by topping up the income of those at the bottom of the income distribution. The only people who lose out as a result of cutting tax credits are those at the bottom of the income distribution, therefore increasing the gap between high- and low-income earners and worsening inequality. ⓐ This worsening of income inequality can be illustrated on the diagram below, with the Lorenz curve shifting further away from the line of equality.

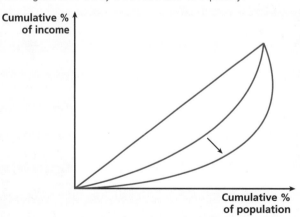

The Gini coefficient is essentially moving closer to 1, with more individuals pushed into relative poverty as a result of these policy reforms (more individuals will be living off an income of less than 50% of median income). **b**

However, the extent to which cutting tax credits will widen inequality in this way depends upon whether this policy is offset by the impact of raising the personal income tax allowance. By increasing the amount of money individuals can earn without paying tax, those at the bottom of the income distribution will get to keep a higher proportion of their income as disposable income, with some low-paid individuals taken out of tax entirely. This could partially compensate the loss in tax credits, as individuals have less tax taken off them in the first place. **c**

Raising the rate at which tax credits are withdrawn as income increases could also have damaging effects on the incentive to work. This essentially means individuals on low incomes who lose tax credits as their income rises face very high marginal tax rates, which could create a poverty trap, whereby individuals are not incentivised to increase their hours of work or more into higher-paid jobs because they will not end up much better off from doing so. This can create poverty in the long term as it means individuals are permanently reliant on support from the government, rather than transitioning into higher-wage employment which enables them to move up the income distribution. **d** In order for the government to avoid this disincentive it may therefore be more effective to make cuts to out-of-work rather than in-work benefits, although this does come with the risk of increasing levels of absolute poverty. **e**

It could instead be argued that these policy measures will actually work to reduce inequality and poverty, particularly through the implementation of the Living Wage. Under the current system, individuals are stuck in a poverty trap, wary of entering the labour market or reducing their working hours because the wages offered are not high enough to make them sufficiently better off from engaging in more labour market activity. By forcing firms to pay workers higher wages this will increase incentives to work, helping those in absolute and relative poverty by incentivising those in absolute poverty into work and raising the income of those in relative poverty who are already in work. **f** Considered alongside reform to tax credits, this seems like an appropriate set of government policies, as they shift the burden of pushing up the income of those at the bottom of the distribution of income from the government to the employer, saving the government money that is needed to reduce the deficit and eventually provide further funds to invest in education, which can have a powerful impact on reducing poverty in the long term. **g**

However, this analysis assumes that firms respond positively to the Living Wage. In this globalised world it may be that firms decide to relocate to countries with lower labour costs. This would cause inequality and poverty to rise as a result of increasing unemployment. **h**

In judgement, these policy measures should if anything have the effect of decreasing inequality and poverty, as the higher wages individuals will be earning as a result of the Living Wage, coupled with the lower taxes they will be paying as a result of the increase in the personal allowance, should more than offset any reductions low-paid individuals receive in tax credits. However, this will only be true in the long term — in the transition period when individuals find their tax credits withdrawn before the Living Wage has risen to its target level, inequality may worsen. 🔲

ⓔ **18/25 marks awarded.** 🄰 The student offers strong analysis of the reasons why cutting tax credits will worsen inequality, explaining how these cuts will affect low earners only. 🄱 The technical theories of the Lorenz curve and the Gini coefficient are used to support this analysis, with a graphic illustration presented of the impact of tax credit cuts on inequality and poverty. 🄲 This point is then well evaluated, with the student recognising that tax credit cuts may be offset by the increase in the personal allowance. 🄳 A further strong analysis point is offered in terms of the impact increasing the taper rate on tax credits withdrawal will have on incentives to work, creating long-term relative poverty. 🄴 An alternative method of achieving reductions in government expenditure is considered in the form of cutting out-of-work benefits. While the limitation of such a policy is recognised, more could be done to explain why absolute poverty is likely to rise in these circumstances. 🄵 The student goes on to consider the implications of implementing the Living Wage and presents strong analysis of why this will reduce both absolute and relative poverty. 🄶 An excellent point is made explaining how the policy measures in combination will provide the government with more funds to tackle the long-term causes of poverty by improving educational attainment. 🄷 The idea that the Living Wage could cause firms to relocate acts as an important limitation to the analysis. 🄸 The judgement summarises the prior arguments to reach a neat conclusion, although it is perhaps lacking mention of the fact that there will inevitably be some winners and some losers as a result of this policy change.

Student B

A major cause of inequality and poverty is the lack of affordable childcare. This restricts parents' participation in the labour market, often resulting in them being out of work because they cannot find a job that fits around their responsibilities to look after their children or in them being in part-time employment, which is traditionally low paid. 🄰 By improving the availability of affordable childcare, parents should find it easier to participate more fully in the labour market, enabling them to engage in full-time employment and therefore reducing income inequality. Moreover, if children from disadvantaged backgrounds have access to better quality early years education, this will improve their earnings potential in the long term. 🄱

However, this argument rests on parents with young children having the relevant skills to be able to take up higher-paid employment. For many low-paid workers, their lack of skill, rather than childcare responsibilities, is the biggest barrier to them being able to increase their earnings; improving the availability of childcare does nothing to address this problem. c

It is important to note that these policy reforms are unlikely to have an impact on absolute poverty. These reforms are primarily designed to target those who are in work; for individuals unable to find a job, there is unlikely to be any change in their circumstances. d

Moreover, the policies do nothing to address wealth inequality. This is a major cause of inequality, as wealth inequality can also lead to income inequality because those with large stocks of wealth are able to generate income off these assets. e

e 6/25 marks awarded. a The answer starts with an explanation of why a lack of affordable childcare causes poverty and inequality. b Reasonable analysis is presented of why improving childcare provision should solve this problem, although a clearer link to reducing poverty could be made in terms of rising wages. c The student offers reasonable evaluation of this point by explaining how improved childcare will not necessarily lead to increased wages at the bottom of the income distribution. d A sensible point on absolute poverty is offered, but more could have been done with this — it could have been noted that the rising living wage may actually worsen absolute poverty because it makes it even harder for those out of work to find a job. e A further reasonable point is made recognising that the policies are more targeted at income inequality than wealth inequality. However, the answer suffers from not addressing directly the impact of the policies mentioned in the question — for example, there is no discussion surrounding the impact of the cuts to tax credits. The student also fails to reach a judgement in this answer.

■ A-level Themes in Economics Section A

Multiple-choice questions

Question 1

Which of the following is not a measure of economic development?

A   GNI per capita

B   Gini coefficient

C   Human Development Index

D   Genuine Progress Indicator

Question 2

The primary purpose of the World Bank is to:

A   Provide short-term financial assistance to countries suffering from balance of payments deficits.

B   Promote free trade by encouraging the removal of barriers to trade between countries.

C   Provide long-term funding for projects that promote economic development.

D   Broker agreements between countries to determine a common interest rate.

Question 3

Neoclassical and Keynesian economists disagree on the workings of the macroeconomy because:

A   Neoclassicists believe the economy will converge rapidly to a natural rate of output, while Keynesians believe there will be a range of values over which the aggregate supply curve is upward sloping.

B   Neoclassicists believe in the principle of the 'Invisible Hand', while Keynesians believe in methodological individualism.

C   Neoclassicists argue that prices are 'sticky', while Keynesians argue that prices and wages are flexible.

D   Neoclassicists believe unemployment is caused by deficiencies in aggregate demand, while Keynesians believe unemployment is caused by imperfections in markets.

Question 4

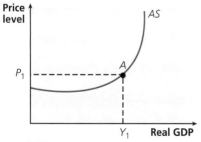

An economy operating at point *A* can be described as:

A Having a positive output gap.

B Operating productively and efficiently.

C Being at the recovery stage of the economic cycle.

D Having a negative output gap.

Question 5

The Heckscher–Ohlin theory proposes that:

A Economic integration is crucial in explaining patterns of world trade.

B Countries should specialise in the production of goods which intensively utilise the factors of production they have an abundant supply of.

C Individuals would prefer to hold their wealth in money as opposed to other assets because money is the most liquid asset.

D A stable growth path is dependent on the savings ratio and the productivity of capital.

Answers and rationale

Question 1

A GNI per capita is a measure of economic development, as average income determines the goods and services consumers can afford to buy and therefore provides an important indication as to material standards of living in the country. The higher the average income, the higher the government's tax revenue and the savings rate are likely to be — both of these are important in generating economic development.

B *Correct answer.* The Gini coefficient measures the degree of income inequality in a country. While improving the distribution of income is an important macroeconomic objective, the Gini coefficient does not provide enough information to assess a country's state of economic development. For example, one country may have a Gini coefficient closer to zero than another country but be at a much earlier stage of economic development, with the low Gini coefficient simply reflecting a relatively even distribution of very low national income in the country.

C The Human Development Index (HDI) provides a composite measure of economic development, incorporating average income, educational attainment and life expectancy. It is measured on a 0–1 scale: the closer the HDI value is to 1, the more economically developed the country is.

D Comprised of 26 components covering economic, environmental and social factors, the Genuine Progress Indicator (GPI) provides a broader measure of economic development than that offered by the HDI.

Question 2

A This is the role of the IMF, which tends to attach reform conditions to any financial assistance it provides.

B This is the role of the WTO.

C *Correct answer.* The World Bank provides loans at commercial interest rates on projects traditional lenders would consider too risky to provide finance for.

D Interest rates are not set at a global level but are instead determined by central banks, such as the Bank of England in the UK and the European Central Bank in the eurozone.

Question 3

A *Correct answer.* Neoclassicists argue that output is always at the natural rate, meaning changes in aggregate demand will have no impact on real output. Keynesians argue the government has a greater role to play in stimulating the macroeconomy, observing disequilibrium unemployment as a solvable phenomenon.

B While neoclassical economists do indeed agree with Adam Smith's 'invisible hand' principle that markets left to adjust without intervention will reach equilibrium, the concept of methodological interventionism is attributed to the Austrian school of thought, believing that macroeconomics needs to recognise the importance of subjective individual decision making.

C The reverse of this is true. Neoclassicists argue that prices and wages are fully flexible as markets adjust instantaneously while Keynesians argue prices are 'sticky'. For example, Keynesians argue that wages are sticky downwards because workers will not accept cuts in their nominal wage.

D The reverse is true — Keynesians believe in the principle of demand-deficient unemployment, while neoclassicists argue that there will be a constant natural rate of unemployment.

Question 4

A A positive output gap occurs when actual output exceeds potential output.

B Productive efficiency occurs when an economy is operating at full capacity — this is where actual output is equal to potential output and there is no spare capacity.

C It is not possible to tell what phase of the economic cycle an economy is at without some indication of what is happening to GDP over time — this static *AD/AS* diagram illustrates GDP at only one point in time.

D *Correct answer.* There is a negative output gap here, as potential output exceeds actual output — there is spare capacity in the economy.

Question 5

A While Heckscher–Ohlin argues trade is determined by comparative advantage, in reality trade is distorted by trade deals between countries. Certain countries with comparative advantage are unable to exploit this in some instances because of protectionist measures imposed by potential trading partners.

B *Correct answer.* The Heckscher–Ohlin theory is a theory of international trade explaining that comparative advantage is derived from the relative factor endowments of different countries, with countries enjoying a comparative advantage in the production of goods which intensively utilise those factors of production which are in plentiful supply in that country.

C This is the liquidity preference theory, which can be used to explain why the demand curve for money is downward sloping, as the cost of holding money increases the higher the interest rate.

D This is the Harrod–Domar model, which argues that improving the savings ratio must be a crucial objective of developing countries, as high levels of savings are required to be transformed into investment in the productive capital that is needed to generate high levels of economic growth.

■A-level Themes in Economics Section B

Data-response

Romania: a transitioning economy

Following the collapse of the Soviet Union, countries in Eastern Europe entered a phase of transition from operating command to market economies. The International Monetary Fund (IMF) and the World Bank were influential in proposing strategies to enable a successful transition, having observed the policies used with varying success in Latin America in the 1980s. These policies included the privatisation of state-owned enterprises, the elimination of subsidies and the removal of price controls.

In Romania, despite the execution of communist leader Nicolae Ceausescu in 1989, political power continued to be in the hands of former communists throughout the early 1990s. Political feuding following the election of a centrist government in 1996, followed by the return of the left in 2000, meant that Romania's transition to a market economy was initially limited, certainly in comparison with countries such as Poland, which adopted many of the policy measures recommended by the IMF and the World Bank. The growth rates of selected transition economies can be seen in the figure.

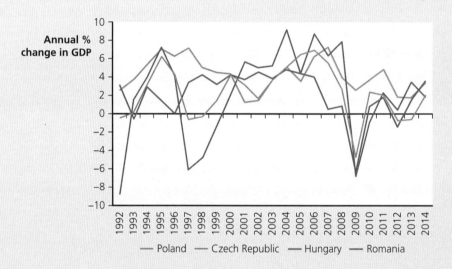

Election of a centrist government in 2004 accelerated Romania's transition. Foreign aid helped to contribute towards a structural reform agenda with a particular focus on the energy and transport sectors, where the government sought to enhance competition and attract the private capital needed to boost competitiveness. Alongside a broader programme of privatisation and market-based reforms, this was successful in delivering consistently high economic growth rates in Romania, excusing the deep recession experienced in 2008 as a result of the global financial crisis.

Greater focus has also been placed in recent years on improving the social security system in Romania. Access to healthcare, which was previously heavily skewed in favour of the wealthy, has been improved, while wider reforms of the pension system have taken place in an attempt to reduce poverty rates among the elderly. These measures have been successful in significantly reducing Romania's poverty rate, which declined dramatically from 36% in 2000 to 5.7% in 2008.

Since the 2004 reforms the savings ratio has been increasing at a steady rate. Table 2 provides data on how the savings rate has changed over time in Romania in comparison with the Human Development Index (HDI) for the country. The HDI is a key measure of economic development. It is interesting to note that the savings rate in Romania is significantly below the 50% savings rate observed in China, which has seen rapid economic growth for more than a decade.

Table 2 Savings and HDI in Romania

Year	Savings rate (%)	HDI
1980	34	0.685
1990	20.80	0.703
2000	14.10	0.706
2005	13.10	0.75
2010	19.80	0.779
2011	21.60	0.782
2012	21.90	0.782
2013	22.30	0.785

Perhaps the most significant landmark in recent years came in 2007, when Romania was admitted into the EU. One key advantage of this is that it has given the country access to international financial markets, enabling it to borrow the funds the Harrod–Domar model proposes are essential in achieving economic development.

Romania has also benefited from being part of the EU's single market. Free trade between member states has enabled Romanian citizens and firms to benefit from trade creation, while trade has also been diverted from Romanian's competitors outside of the EU towards Romanian firms, which have benefited from protectionist measures being lifted.

Romania is blessed with extensive natural resources, a productive agricultural sector and the potential for strong growth in industry and tourism, all of which suggest encouraging prospects for the economy. However, with a third of workers still employed in agriculture and the poverty rate still being the highest in the EU, there is clearly still much work to do before these prospects are realised.

(a) State two functions of the International Monetary Fund. (2 marks)

@ Identify two functions of the IMF. This question does not require you to explain any of the factors.

(b) Using the chart, compare and contrast the economic growth experienced by Romania with other transitioning economies. (2 marks)

@ Begin by looking for the similarities and differences between Romania's growth rate and that experienced in other countries. Identify these by quoting the data directly.

(c) The case study refers to the greater focus placed on improving the social security system in Romania in recent years. Use a diagram to illustrate the impact of such measures on the distribution of income in Romania. (4 marks)

@ Draw a Lorenz curve diagram clearly illustrating the impact on the distribution of income of improvements in the social security system. Make sure you refer to this diagram in your answer and explain clearly how changes in social security will impact upon the distribution of income.

(d) Evaluate the effectiveness of overseas development assistance (ODA) in promoting economic growth and development. (8 marks)

ⓔ Aim to make two arguments explaining why overseas development assistance may be effective in promoting economic development. Evaluate these arguments by recognising their limitations or the conditions under which they may not hold. The answer should end with a clearly supported judgement where you explain whether you believe ODA is effective in promoting economic growth and development.

(e) Trade creation and trade diversion will occur as a result of Romania joining the European Union. Using a relevant diagram(s), evaluate the consequences to Romania and other nations of Romania joining the European Union. (15 marks)

ⓔ Start by drawing diagrams illustrating the impact of trade diversion and trade creation. Using your diagrams, analyse the winners and losers of Romania joining the EU. Go on to evaluate your analysis by considering circumstances under which your analysis might not hold. End by reaching a supported judgement which clearly identifies who the winners and losers are.

(f) Using the data in Table 2, compare how the savings rate and the Human Development Index have changed over time in Romania. Explain whether the relationship between the two sets of data is what you would expect. (4 marks)

ⓔ Look for the key trends in how the savings rate and the HDI have developed over time and explain any relationship that exists between these two datasets. Then consider what relationship you would expect to see according to economic theory and explain whether the data support this.

(g) One of the most significant advantages to Romania of joining the European Union was the improved access it gave the country to international financial markets. Evaluate the role of international financial markets in developing countries achieving economic growth and development. (15 marks)

ⓔ A two-sided answer is required here that recognises the harms a National Living Wage could cause to international competitiveness while considering reasons why these harms may not be particularly significant. You could also consider why international competitiveness may actually improve as a result of this policy. Be sure to explain within your answer what is meant by international competitiveness and conclude by providing a supported judgement which is clearly focused on the question.

Student A

(a) One function of the IMF is to provide countries with short-term loans to help them deal with balance of payments deficits. Another function is to support countries in overcoming an economic crisis by coordinating the actions of several countries to provide loans, which often have reforming conditions attached to them.

ⓔ **2/2 marks awarded.** The student clearly identifies two functions of the IMF — the traditional role in helping with balance of payments adjustments and the more recent role of providing more significant financial support in the event of an economic crisis.

(b) Romania took longer to experience consistent periods of economic growth following the collapse of the Soviet Union than the other transition economies. Romania experienced a deep recession in 2008 similar to that experienced by the other transition economies; the exception in this instance was Poland, which continued to grow in 2008.

ⓔ 1/2 marks awarded. The different growth path experienced by Romania following the collapse of the Soviet Union is correctly identified, as is the fact that Romania experienced a similar decline in output in 2008 as two of the other transitioning economies. However, the answer lacks specific reference to the data — for example, while in 1997 Poland's economy was growing by more than 6%, Romania's economy was contracting by 6%.

(c)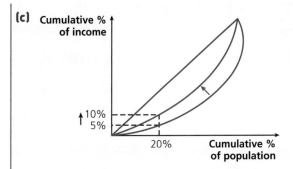

Improving the social security system will raise the post-tax income of those at the bottom of the income distribution, as it will involve those in poverty receiving a variety of benefits, such as increased pension entitlement. This will serve to shift the Lorenz curve closer to the line of equality, as illustrated in the diagram. This means that the distribution of income has improved — for example, the bottom quintile of earners used to account for only 5% of national income but now account for 10%.

ⓔ 4/4 marks awarded. An excellent answer which clearly explains why income inequality will be reduced as a result of improvements in social security. The diagram is accurate and well integrated into the answer, with a good example showing the student understands how to interpret Lorenz curves.

(d) Overseas development assistance can significantly aid economic development in a country by providing the funds needed to carry out large infrastructure projects. For example, in Romania there was a need to improve the transportation network, which can be crucial in aiding economic development as it can significantly enhance productivity in a range of sectors. However, the Romanian government is unlikely to have sufficient finance to fund such a project; overseas development assistance can provide this much-needed injection of funds, allowing infrastructure to improve. With better transport networks industry will be able to develop — in fact, it may even incentivise multinationals to locate in the country, which will generate employment. All of this is likely to enhance economic growth.

However, this depends upon whether the funds from the donor country need to be paid back. Many developing nations found themselves with a crippling debt burden — if the country finds itself having to pay back large loans to developed nations this can actually hinder economic development, as a high proportion of GDP is spent making debt interest payments.

Support from developed nations can also be crucial in ensuring aid is well targeted. Many developing nations lack the entrepreneurship needed for economic development; developed countries therefore have a role to play in advising on the development of infrastructure. However, this depends upon the system of governance in the recipient country. Historically, aid has been poorly used by developing nations because of corrupt political regimes — if this is the case, they simply find themselves with greater debt and no improvement in infrastructure.

Overall, overseas development assistance clearly can be important in promoting growth and development, as it can provide developing countries with a crucial inflow of funds. The fact though that many countries have received such assistance but remain poor demonstrates that a number of other circumstances also need to exist alongside this assistance in order for it to be effective.

ⓔ 7/8 marks awarded. The student offers strong analysis of why ODA can be crucial in allowing infrastructure to develop, which is important in enabling a country to achieve economic growth. This point is well evaluated by noting that the debt burden that can result from taking on assistance from developed countries can hinder economic development in the long term. A further analysis point is made highlighting the role developed economies can play in supporting developing nations channel funds effectively, subject to the important condition that the recipient of aid has a strong system of governance. A clear judgement is reached, although more detail on the other conditions needed for aid to result in development would strengthen the answer.

(e)

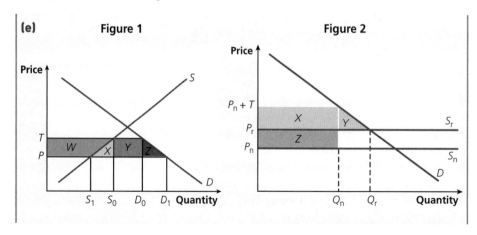

Figure 1   Figure 2

Joining the EU means Romania will face no tariffs or quotas when selling to other nations in the EU, with common external tariffs imposed on non-member nations. **a** Romanian consumers are likely to benefit from the country joining the European Union, as illustrated in Figure 1, which shows the market for a good or service which Romania imports from another EU country. Before Romania entered the EU, tariffs were imposed, meaning consumers paid a price of T for the good. When Romania enters the EU the tariff is removed from the foreign producer, enabling consumers to purchase the good at a cheaper price of P. This improves consumers' standard of living, as they can afford to purchase more goods and services. The increase in consumer surplus which results is represented by area $W + X + Y + Z$. **b**

Moreover, in Figure 2 it is possible to see the gains which are enjoyed by Romanian producers as a result of trade diversion. In this diagram, assume the market is for an agricultural product in another EU country. Prior to becoming a member of the EU, you can see that Romania were simply unable to produce the products as cheaply (at a price of P_r) as another non-member (at a price of P_n). Given that both countries faced tariffs to export to the EU member, the EU member would not purchase any imports from Romania, but from the other non-member country, as their price with the tariff of $P_n + T$ would be lower than Romania's price with the tariff. However, when Romania joins the EU it now has a competitive advantage over non-member countries, as it is able to sell to EU countries without a tariff. This enables it to sell at a price of P_r — cheaper than the non-member who faces a tariff. This causes trade to be diverted from the non-member towards Romania, with Romanian firms now benefitting from the export of Q_r agricultural products. **c**

However, the extent to which Romanian firms benefit depends upon which industry the firms are operating in. Clearly firms which are now able to export to other EU members, as illustrated in Figure 2, benefit from EU membership. However, domestic firms in industries previously shielded from international competition by tariffs which now face competition from other EU firms will lose out. This is illustrated in Figure 1, where domestic firms find production falling from S_0 to S_1 as a result of other EU firms entering the market, resulting in a loss of producer surplus equal to area W. **d**

Ultimately, Romania will benefit from membership of the European Union. Consumers will unambiguously benefit from greater choice at lower prices and, although some domestic firms may initially suffer from the greater competition which comes from other EU nations, this will in the long run drive efficiency gains and enable Romania to more fully exploit its comparative advantage. The only countries that stand to lose in the long term are those outside of the EU, which could see trade diverted away from them, as experienced by the non-member country in Figure 2. **e**

ⓔ 12/15 marks awarded. ⓐ The answer begins by accurately explaining the changes to trading arrangements that will result from Romania joining the EU. ⓑ Strong analysis is offered of the trade creation diagram, beginning with an explanation of how consumers will benefit from lower prices. ⓒ The explanation of how Romanian firms can benefit from trade diversion is excellent, with a clear technical presentation of how trade will be diverted towards Romania now it is an EU member. ⓓ Strong evaluation of this is offered by considering the extent to which Romanian firms benefit, with the student recognising some Romanian firms stand to gain more than others. ⓔ The judgement is a suitable conclusion as it weighs up both sides of the analysis presented so far, although the answer would have benefited from a deeper consideration of the impacts on non-members.

(f) The savings rate fell between 1980 and 2005 but has been steadily on the rise since then. The Human Development Index has been increasing steadily over the entire period, suggesting economic development has been occurring in Romania. The Harrod–Domar model suggests there should be a positive relationship between the savings rate and economic development. This relationship does not hold between 1980 and 2005 — the savings rate is falling while the HDI is rising. This is surprising. The relationship does hold from 2005 onwards though, with HDI rising in line with increases in the savings rate.

ⓔ 3/4 marks awarded. This is a good technical answer which correctly identifies the trends and also identifies the periods in which the trends are both consistent and inconsistent with economic theory. For full marks the student should have offered some insight into why the relationship did not hold between 1980 and 2005 — for example, they could have pointed out that the Romanian economy was in transition to a market economy during this period, meaning there were a number of other factors which would have been influencing development during this time.

(g) The Harrod–Domar model demonstrates that the limited productive capacity of developing nations is often a key barrier to their development, arguing that high levels of investment are needed to achieve the growth in the productive capacity that is essential for economic development to occur. A high savings rate is a route to achieving a stable growth path because savings can provide the funds necessary to invest beyond the level of simply replacing depreciating capital, enabling a genuine expansion in the economy's productive capacity and therefore an increase in real incomes. However, low incomes in developing countries tend to mean the savings ratio is too low to generate sufficient funds for investment, meaning there is an important role for international financial markets to play. ⓐ By borrowing from abroad, developing countries are able to gain access to funds they simply couldn't generate domestically, which can then be used to invest in the infrastructure needed to expand the economy's productive capacity. Countries such as South Korea and Singapore have used international financial markets in this way to good effect to achieve rapid economic development. ⓑ

However, this assumes that the funds borrowed on international financial markets are used in a way that promotes economic development. Political corruption in many developing nations means such borrowing has often been used to fund vanity projects which have had no impact on the productive capacity of the economy. Instead, this borrowing simply creates a debt crisis in the country that hinders development in the future, with an increasingly large proportion of GDP being dedicated to making debt interest repayments. **c**

Moreover, the undeveloped nature of financial markets in developing countries means there are often not the institutions available to successfully transform savings to investment. This means saving often takes place outside of financial institutions and borrowers cannot get access to the funds needed to undertake investment. International financial markets provide the opportunity for developing nations to benefit from significant inflows of foreign direct investment, providing the money needed for infrastructure development. **d** However, this assumes developing nations are able to attract inflows of foreign direct investment. While being members of the EU has certainly increased FDI flows between members, this finance has often been flowing into the more developed economies of countries such as the UK and Germany, where investors consider they can get a better and more guaranteed return. Therefore, access to international financial markets actually has the potential to divert funds away from developing nations towards the more developed nations. **e**

In conclusion, access to international financial markets is essential in promoting economic development. Providing funds are used wisely, they enable investment to take place that simply wouldn't be possible without having access to the funds provided on international financial markets, enabling economic growth to occur. **f**

e 11/15 marks awarded. a The answer begins by justifying the need for high levels of investment to achieve economic development and outlines why the savings ratio in developing countries tends to be insufficient to generate this investment. **b** There is strong analysis of how international financial markets can be used to provide the funds which enable investment in expanding the economy's productive capacity. **c** The limitations of this are well evaluated, with good consideration of how the funds may be used inappropriately and then create a debt crisis for the country. **d** The student goes on to explain how developing countries require access to international financial markets because of the weak state of their own domestic financial markets. **e** Strong evaluation of this point is offered, with recognition that developing countries often struggle to attract sufficient inflows of FDI. **f** The answer reaches a clear conclusion, but this could be better justified.

Student B

(a) The IMF acts as a banker to the central banks. In this respect it controls government budgets and the interest rate.

e **1/2 marks awarded.** Credit is awarded for recognising the IMF acts as a banker to central banks, but this is only to the extent that it can provide short-term finance to central banks. It does not have wider control over a country's interest rate or budget decisions.

(b) Romania experienced a more volatile growth path than the other transitioning economies. Romania grew by 9% in 2004 — the highest growth rate experienced by any of the economies during the period — while the economy shrank by more than 8% in 1992, which is the biggest contraction evidenced.

e **1/2 marks awarded.** Recognising that growth in Romania was more volatile than in other nations gets credit, but the student should compare the pattern of growth between the countries, not just individual growth rates.

(c)
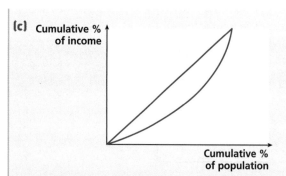

Social security payments are targeted at low-income households, which will increase their income and reduce income inequality. This is illustrated in the diagram.

e **1/4 marks awarded.** The student correctly identifies that social security payments will raise the income of those at the bottom of the income distribution, but this is a static analysis with a diagram that simply illustrates income inequality, not a reduction in income inequality.

(d) Overseas development assistance is ineffective because such aid is often 'tied'. Developed nations often grant aid to countries on the proviso that they get something in return. The recipient country could, for example, be required to purchase imports from the donor country at high prices or be forced to sell exports to the donor country at below market rates. This can offset any benefits that come from receiving the assistance in the first place.

e **2/8 marks awarded.** The student offers reasonable analysis of a key criticism of ODA. However, no positive case is made in favour of ODA — there is no explanation of how ODA could be seen to promote economic growth and development.

> **(e)** When Romania joins the EU, domestic producers will benefit. This is because they will be able to sell without any barriers to other EU member countries, making their goods more price competitive. **a** This will increase demand for the products and increase exports, which is good for jobs, growth and the profitability of Romanian firms. **b** Consumers will also benefit because they get access to cheaper imports. This is likely to increase their material standards of living, as they can afford to purchase more goods and services than before. **c**
>
> However, the extent to which Romanian firms benefit depends upon which firms are being considered. While firms whose exports increase will benefit, firms that find themselves outcompeted from imports from other EU countries and therefore lose domestic demand as a result will lose out. **d**

e **3/15 marks awarded.** **a** The student correctly identifies that joining the European Union would result in Romanian firms being able to engage in free trade with other EU members. **b** Reasonable analysis is then offered of how this will increase exports, but links in the analysis are missing, as there is no clear explanation of how this brings about the increased employment mentioned in the answer. **c** The positive impact on consumers is also noted, although the answer could be improved by explaining why imports become cheaper. **d** A limited attempt at evaluation is made by recognising that not all firms in Romania will share in the gains from trade. The answer is missing technical analysis of the gains from trade, as no trade creation or trade diversion diagrams are included. The impact upon other countries of Romania's membership is also not considered.

> **(f)** There should be a positive correlation between the savings rate and the HDI — the higher the level of saving in the economy, the more potential there is for development to take place. The data support this pattern — in 2005 when the savings rate is only 13.1%, the HDI is 0.75, while when the savings rate increases to 22.3% in 2013, the HDI increases to 0.785.

e **2/4 marks awarded.** The student correctly identifies what economic theory suggests the relationship between the savings rate and the HDI should be and finds some supporting evidence for this in the data. However, they ignore the period between 1980 and 2005 when the expected relationship clearly doesn't hold. It is important to avoid simply looking for the pattern you would like to see when examining data.

(g) Access to international financial markets will provide the funds needed for investment, which would not otherwise be available in the domestic economy. a However, evidence from the case study suggests that having sufficient funds for investment does not necessarily result in economic development being achieved. In the 1980s Romania had a much higher savings ratio than it did in the early 2000s and yet the HDI was much lower then. This demonstrates that the funds generated by international financial markets are not that significant in promoting economic development — ultimately, these funds were available domestically in the 1980s because of the high savings ratio and yet economic development did not occur, suggesting other factors are more important in determining economic development. b For example, the competency and outlook of the government is crucial in determining the country's ability to successfully transform savings into investment — it is the transition to market economics that has been most critical in enabling Romania to develop. Moreover, if countries have insufficient human capital to make effective use of the more sophisticated physical capital that results from FDI then international capital markets will be ineffective in achieving economic development. c

Also, access to international financial markets can serve to worsen inequality, in doing so making a negative contribution to economic development. This is because FDI is often targeted towards particular groups of individuals or businesses in urban areas. Rural areas can therefore be left behind, increasing the income gap between urban and rural areas and doing nothing to overcome rural poverty. d Therefore, the extent to which access to international financial markets promotes economic development depends upon how wide this access is — if rural villages are able to access the finance, perhaps in the form of microfinance, then it is likely that it will make a more positive contribution towards economic development in the country. e

e 7/15 marks awarded. a The answer recognises that international financial markets provide the funds needed for investment, but it lacks an explanation of why investment is so critical to economic development — reference to the Harrod–Domar model would be worthwhile. b A good analysis is offered detailing the limitations of international financial markets in promoting economic development. c Alternative factors that are important in determining economic development are identified and well explained. d A good explanation is offered of how FDI can worsen inequality. e Reasonable evaluation of this is offered by questioning the extent to which FDI flows filter out to rural areas, although more detail on the role of microfinance would have been beneficial. Ultimately, the answer needs to do more in setting out the clear benefits of international financial markets to developing economies.

Knowledge check answers

1 The average income level is broadly the same in the USA on both measures but is double in Mozambique using the PPP measure in comparison with the US dollar measure. While still demonstrating a significant gap in living standards between the two countries, the gap is clearly not as big once relative purchasing power is taken into account.

2 Bilateral aid is assistance given by one country to another. Multilateral aid is channelled through organisations such as the World Bank or the UN and usually comes with conditions of particular policy reforms.

3 There is very little absolute poverty because of government policies such as the minimum wage and the welfare state. Relative poverty is therefore more common.

4 Japan, UK, USA, Brazil.

5 Corporation tax, capital gains tax, inheritance tax, national insurance contributions.

6 Unemployment would have to be increased in order to reduce inflation. If the economy was then at point D and inflation was lower than expected, expectations would adjust and the Phillips curve would shift back in to PC_0. This would mean the equilibrium position of point A would be reached again. The length of time this adjustment in expectations takes will determine how costly the additional unemployment needed to reach this position is.

7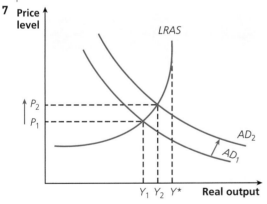

Implementing expansionary fiscal policy by, for example, cutting the basic rate of income tax will cause the aggregate demand curve to shift out from AD_1 to AD_2. This will result in some of the previously unemployed factors of production being employed, increasing real output from Y_1 to Y_2 and reducing the size of the negative output gap from (Y^*-Y_1) to (Y^*-Y_2).

8 FDI is investment undertaken in one country by companies based in other countries. Companies that undertake such investment are known as multinational corporations, whose production activities are conducted in more than one country.

9 Terms of trade = $122 \div 114 \times 100 = 107$. The terms of trade have improved by 7% — the same volume of exports can purchase 7% more imports in 2016 than in 2006.

10 In order to reduce the reliance on primary sector production an LDC may attempt to shift its pattern of comparative advantage towards the manufacturing sector. This will, however, take time. If in the short run the newly formed manufacturing sector were exposed to international competition, it would be unlikely to be able to survive. It therefore needs a period of protectionism to enable the sector to develop before it can engage successfully in international competition.

11 Quotas guarantee a reduction in imports in a way that tariffs do not. Tariffs indirectly try to control the volume of imports through increasing their price, but if the demand for imports is price inelastic, they will not reduce the volume of imports. Through putting a specific limit on the quantity of imports, quotas therefore guarantee a reduction in the volume of imports.

12 While the domestic firms in Figure 16 lost out because they were operating in an industry in which another member state enjoyed a comparative advantage, domestic firms operating in industries in which they enjoy comparative advantage are likely to gain as they will be able to export without tariffs being imposed to other member states. More generally, being part of a customs union exposes domestic firms to greater international competition, which could lead to long-term improvements in productivity and competitiveness.

13 Ideally the country would like to implement expansionary monetary policy, cutting interest rates to stimulate aggregate demand and move the country out of recession. However, in a monetary union the country does not have independent control of monetary policy. It could be the case that other countries in the union are in the boom phase of the economic cycle, meaning the central bank decides to pursue contractionary monetary policy despite one country being in recession.

14 With a single currency it is easier to compare prices between member states as all goods and services will be priced in the same currency. This enables firms to more easily identify the cheapest places from which to buy inputs and consumers to identify the cheapest places from which to buy their goods and services.

15 Money would no longer be a store of value because, for example, £1,000 today would be worth next to nothing in a year when the inflation rate was 2000%. It would then stop becoming a means of deferred payment because individuals would not be prepared to accept the promise of money in the future in return for goods and services now, because it would be impossible to predict how much the good was worth in future prices. With the general price

level increasing by the day it would no longer be an accurate unit of account. All of these reasons mean money would stop being accepted as a medium of exchange.

16 Liquidity ratio = £100 ÷ £350 = 0.286.
Credit multiplier = 1 ÷ 0.286 = 3.5.
Total increase in bank lending when government increases money supply by £5 million = £5,000,000 × 3.5 = £17.5 million.

17

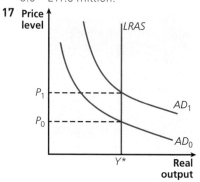

When the money supply increases, firms and individuals find themselves with excess cash balances and will choose to spend some of these, increasing aggregate demand. When the aggregate demand curve shifts to the right, this simply causes the rate of inflation to increase, as the aggregate supply curve is perfectly inelastic at the natural rate of output.

18 There is no collateral against which overdraft and credit card debt is secured, which is why the interest rate charged is higher than on mortgages. There are also no fixed repayment terms with such borrowing and borrowers have flexibility over how much money to borrow and when they borrow it, which is why the rate of interest is higher than on personal loans.

19 Overseas assistance is often tied to a particular trade deal designed to benefit the donor nation. While MNC investment can be valuable, these companies repatriate their profits. International borrowing can help in the short term but will eventually need to be repaid — this can create an unsustainable debt burden for LDCs.

20 Different goods and services are included in the baskets — for example, the CPI excludes mortgage interest payments, which the RPI includes. The CPI includes all households in the UK, whereas the RPI excludes the highest and lowest earners. The RPI is calculated using an arithmetic mean, while the CPI is calculated using a geometric mean.

Index